THE 100 one hundred greatest Cricketers

NICK BROWNLEE

WITH AN INTRODUCTION BY
PETER BAXTER

generation
PUBLICATIONS

"Thanks to Jane, the Number One Greatest partner in the world."

Written by Nick Brownlee

Designed by Robert Kelland and Adrian Waddington

With thanks to
Phil McNeill, Eve Cossins, Mark Crossland and Deanne Pearson;
and to Julie Foster and Rob Brown at Colour Systems

Special thanks to Peter Baxter, Jonathan Agnew, Henry Blofeld, Bill Frindall and Christopher Martin-Jenkins

Published by David Crowe and Mark Peacock

First published in Great Britain in 1999 by Generation Publications
11-12 Tottenham Mews, London W1P 9PJ

generationgroup@btconnect.com

Text copyright © Generation Publications 1999

Production by Mike Powell & Associates (01494 676891)
Origination by Colour Systems Ltd. London
Printed and bound in Spain by Bookprint, S.L.,Barcelona

The photographs in the book are from Allsport, with thanks to Rob Harborne and Mark Goldsmith,
and Phil Burnham-Richards at Hulton Getty;
from Patrick Eagar, with thanks to Lynda Cole and Jan Traylen;
and from Corbis, with thanks to Lizzie Assad

....

Page 1: Ian Botham takes on Geoff Lawson at Headingley in 1981

Page 2: Brian Lara in Melbourne, 1998

Page 3: Don Bradman

Contents

Introduction and Experts' XIs	6	Clive Lloyd	55	Alec Bedser	88
Don Bradman	12	Curtly Ambrose	56	Ted Dexter	88
W.G. Grace	14	Graeme Pollock	57	Colin Cowdrey	89
Jack Hobbs	16	Greg Chappell	58	Neil Harvey	90
Gary Sobers	18	Richard Hadlee	59	Jeff Thomson	90
Brian Lara	20	Frank Worrell	60	Waqar Younis	91
Ian Botham	22	Rodney Marsh	61	Allan Donald	92
Viv Richards	24	Ray Lindwall	62	Malcolm Marshall	92
Len Hutton	26	Fred Trueman	63	Wes Hall	93
Shane Warne	28	Jim Laker	64	John Reid	94
Wilfred Rhodes	30	David Gower	65	Peter May	94
Wally Hammond	32	Geoffrey Boycott	66	Gordon Greenidge	95
Sunil Gavaskar	33	C.B. Fry	67	Geoff Howarth	96
Sachin Tendulkar	34	Brian Statham	68	Derek Randall	96
Dennis Lillee	35	Bobby Simpson	69	Rohan Kanhai	97
Barry Richards	36	Harold Larwood	70	Javed Miandad	98
S.F. Barnes	37	Douglas Jardine	71	John Snow	98
Michael Holding	38	Aravinda de Silva	72	Bill Ponsford	99
Imran Khan	39	Allan Border	73	Ranjitsinhji	100
Denis Compton	40	Ian Chappell	74	Tony Greig	100
Bill O'Reilly	41	Bert Sutcliffe	75	Bhagwat Chandrasekhar	101
Herbert Sutcliffe	42	Jack Russell	76	Merv Hughes	102
Arthur Shrewsbury	43	Jonty Rhodes	77	Ray Illingworth	102
George Headley	44	Bill Lawry	78	Ken Barrington	103
Richie Benaud	45	Clyde Walcott	79	Maurice Tate	104
Kapil Dev	46	Everton Weekes	80	Bishen Bedi	104
George Lohmann	47	Lance Gibbs	81	Martin Crowe	105
Alan Knott	48	Archie Maclaren	82	Hanif Mohammed	106
Steve Waugh	49	Derek Underwood	83	Sonny Ramadhin	106
Frederick Spofforth	50	Clarrie Grimmett	84	Brian Close	107
Graham Gooch	51	Learie Constantine	85	Mike Brearley	108
Godfrey Evans	52	Wasim Bari	86	Mike Gatting	108
Victor Trumper	53	Bob Willis	86	Alvin Kallicharran	109
Mike Procter	58	Keith Miller	87	TMS 1957-97 Dream Team	110

Introduction

by Peter Baxter

'Silver Billy' Beldam

Who were the best – at their best? How would Grace have coped with Lillee or Warne? Could Lara have dominated Spofforth or O'Reilly? We can never know, of course, but what fun we can have conjuring up such confrontations. Probably sixty or so of any selection of the greatest hundred would find us all in agreement. Those last forty places, though, are the agonising ones and I am sure that people will look at Nick Brownlee's list and protest. "How did what's-his-name get in ahead of thingummy-bob?" will be the indignant cry. So, draw up your own list.

We in the *Test Match Special* commentary box have had enormous fun making an eleven out of the 100 names. Try that as an exercise. You may not agree with Henry Blofeld that from the handful of Test matches that Barry Richards played we can be so sure that he was up there with the greatest. And maybe Jonathan Agnew is older than he looks if he's selected W.G. Grace. Or how could Christopher Martin-Jenkins make Botham twelfth man, I hear you cry – and who is going to tell him? Worse still, who is going to tell Fred Trueman that he's not on the team sheets, either? Now maybe you sympathise with David Graveney.

The fascination of this pastime was shown by the discussion provoked some years ago when John Woodcock of *The Times* drew up his list of 100. Two of the great Hambledon players of the 18th century were there – John Small and 'Silver Billy' Beldham – and Alfred Mynn, 'the Lion of Kent', too. It is fun to imagine their reaction to our modern game as much as how they might have fared in it.

Nick Brownlee has not gone back quite so far into the mists of time but he has produced a spread over the years to encourage all of us to speculate – and that is the stuff of cricket supporters' winter dreams.

PETER BAXTER
Producer in charge of BBC Radio's cricket coverage, and author of World Cup: Cricket's Clash Of The Titans

Peter Baxter

1 J.B. Hobbs
2 S.M. Gavaskar
3 D.G. Bradman
4 I.V.A. Richards
5 E. de C. Weekes
6 G. St A. Sobers
7 A.P.E. Knott
8 S.K. Warne
9 S.F. Barnes
10 D.K. Lillee
11 F.R. Spofforth

PLAYER'S CIGARETTES

O. G. BRADMAN (N. S. WALES).

Baxter's choice: West Indian master blaster Viv Richards follows number three batsman The Don in an awesome eleven that includes just one current player, Australian spinner Shane Warne

Any 'best ever' selection inevitably starts with Bradman at number three. The openers ahead of him may vary; I had huge admiration for Sunil Gavaskar and would loved to have seen Hobbs. Viv Richards, the Master Blaster, was such a destroyer and Everton Weekes was an early hero of mine, though I was tempted by two others: Barry Richards, who was cruelly short of Test appearances, and Victor Trumper, who must have been a joy to watch.

Sobers must be another who gets inked in to most teams early on, even though in my case it keeps out Botham and another cavalier character in Keith Miller. After going for Knott to keep wicket and Shane Warne as my only specialist spinner (I have got Sobers's slow left arm), I started my pace attack with Lillee, after which the choice is more tricky. But they say Barnes was the best ever and they called Spofforth the Demon. That's good enough for me.
— *Peter Baxter*

• The Experts' Eleven •

Henry Blofeld

1 Hobbs
2 B.A. Richards
3 Bradman (captain)
4 Compton
5 I.V.A. Richards
6 Sobers
7 Botham
8 Knott
9 Warne
10 Lillee
11 Barnes

A blend of youth, experience and personal prejudice. Although Barry Richards played in only four Test matches, he made batting look easier than anyone else I ever saw. He would be grateful for the steadying influence of Jack Hobbs. Denis Compton in 1947 and thereabouts was incomparable, while Sydney Barnes must have been just about the best bowler ever. The rest pick themselves. — *Henry Blofeld*

Blowers' choice: Top left: Barry Richards opening for Hampshire with Gordon Greenidge – he would open for Blofeld too. **Above:** Sobers in full cry – he'd come in at number six. **Left:** Denis Compton (1940s), who would bat at number four in an eleven which Bradman would captain and which would include only three specialist bowlers – but two outstanding all-rounders, Botham and Sobers

Assuming that my Greatest XI will be playing on the greatest pitch, I have chosen a balanced attack and nine players who have scored Test match hundreds. With Compton, Miller, Sobers and Evans, the dressing room would never be downbeat. Manager Lord Hawke would ensure that Barnes did not quibble about his expenses. — *Bill Frindall*

Bearded Wonder's choice: Hobbs (above), Barnes and Warne

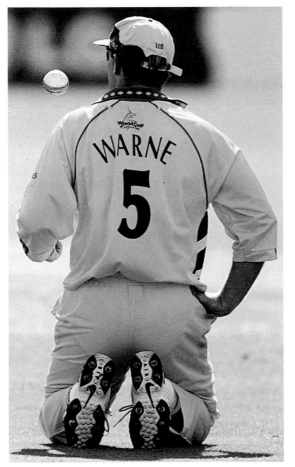

• The Experts' Eleven •

Bill Frindall

1 Hobbs
2 B.A. Richards
3 Bradman (capt)
4 Compton
5 Weekes
6 Sobers
7 K.R. Miller
8 T.G. Evans
9 R.R. Lindwall
10 Warne
11 Barnes

Jonathan Agnew

1 Hutton
2 Hobbs
3 Bradman
4 Lara
5 Viv Richards
6 Grace
7 Botham
8 Knott
9 Lillee
10 Warne
11 Holding

O ne of the most attractive features of cricket is a partnership. This can involve bat or ball, and the team I have chosen is based on superb 'spectator value'. Imagine Bradman batting with Lara – or Richards for that matter – Grace with Botham (there might be a touch of rivalry there too, I fancy, as the two giants tried to outscore each other) and Lillee bowling with Holding. The ECB could charge whatever they wanted to get in to see this team!   – *Jonathan Agnew*

Aggers' choice: Hutton would open and Holding is last man. And in between you get 100 per cent spectator value right through the order

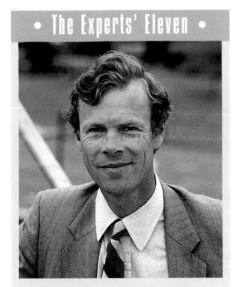

Christopher Martin-Jenkins

1 Hobbs

2 Gavaskar

3 Bradman

4 Lara

5 Sobers

6 Procter

7 Imran Khan

8 Rhodes

9 O'Reilly

10 Evans

11 Barnes

(12th man: Botham)

My perfect side requires courage and impeccable technique from the opening batsmen, genius and attacking flair from three to seven in the order, a brilliant and effervescent wicket-keeper and bowlers to cover every possible eventuality.

Between them this attack could bowl out any opposition for practically nothing on a helpful pitch and, by a combination of speed, swing and guile, find a way through the finest players on even the most perfectly ironed shirt-front.

In the highly unlikely event of all the batsmen having an off day together, there is a Test opener of famous obduracy at number eight and a highly capable number nine, too, whenever he was needed to play seriously.

Eight of the ten fielders are natural athletes who would catch anything above ground. I am not certain that Barnes and O'Reilly would be prepared to fling themselves along the boundary's edge in the modern idiom, but these are champion bowlers, proud, aggressive and indomitable. If they have to use their large feet to stop the ball, so be it.

Just imagine bowling at a line-up starting Hobbs, Gavaskar, Bradman, Lara, Sobers – with Procter and Imran Khan to come: it is the stuff of bowlers' nightmares.

And imagine, as a batsman, seeing off Procter, Imran and Sobers, only to be confronted by Barnes, spitting it in all directions with the flick of a huge hand, O'Reilly, bouncing in with fire in his eyes to hound you with googlies and leg-breaks, and then Rhodes (or Sobers) to tempt and beguile you with flight and timeless craft. – *Christopher Martin-Jenkins*

CMJ's choice: 'Impeccable' Hobbs and Lara genius

Australia captain Don Bradman, right, goes out to toss up with England's Wally Hammond before the 1938 Trent Bridge Test — evidently intending to bat if he wins

Don Bradman

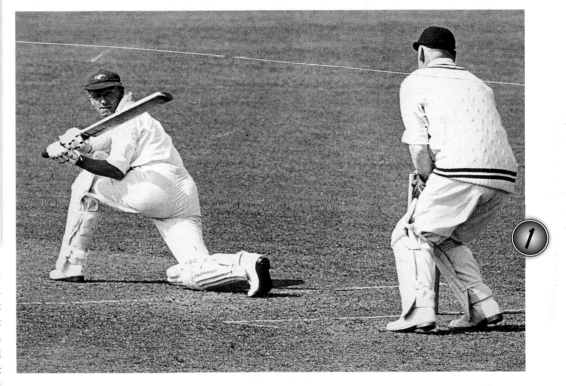

*I*n 1930, the day after Don Bradman, aged 21, had scored 309 runs in the first day of the Headingley Test against England, *The Times*'s leading article was titled "England v Bradman". And that really summed it up. During his 22-year playing career, bowling against Bradman was like bowling against an entire team. He was simply light years ahead in thought and deed of any of his nearest rivals, even those as brilliant as Wally Hammond and George Headley. "Don was too good," said another, Jack Hobbs, "he got too many runs."

Runs were indeed what Bradman was all about. In that 1930 series, he scored a record 974 runs. In 338 first-class innings, he made 117 hundreds with a career average of 95.14; his 52 Tests would have yielded an average of 100 had he not been famously bowled just four short in his last match. It was solely to control Bradman that the 1932 England skipper Douglas Jardine devised Bodyline – and it worked, until the 1934 tour to England in which he scored 304 and 244 in the last two Tests.

Now aged over 90 and living in an suburb of Adelaide, fans still flock to pay homage to the great man. Shy and retiring, Bradman will have none of it. He is quite happy to let his extraordinary record tell the tale.

The centurion of the century: Australia's Don Bradman retired with an average of 99.94

Bradman *factfile*

Born: 27.8.08, New South Wales
Country: Australia
Test career: 52 matches, 6,996 runs, 29 hundreds, average 99.94

2

W.G. Grace

With his fearsome beard and imposing bulk, Dr William Gilbert Grace was a legend not only in his own cricketing lifetime, but of all time. And when it comes to feats of cricketing prowess, top players the world over continue to judge themselves against his achievements with the bat. At the age of 20, he was already being hailed as 'the father of English cricket', and a year later John Lillywhite's *Cricketer's Companion* called him 'the most wonderful cricketer that ever held a bat'. This was all very well for a man who, even at 18, had been dubbed 'the best batsman in England'.

In his heyday, the 11 years between 1869 and 1880, Grace was unstoppable. He topped the English averages for all but two years, and averaged 50. In 1876 he hit two scores of 300 within eight days. He was the first batsman to score 2,000 in a season.

But Grace's legacy to the game is not simply his batting records. It was he who, through his own personal fame, popularised cricket to the masses and to the world. Playing for a travelling XI at Nottingham, he attracted a crowd of over 25,000 to Trent Bridge, and he was among the first players to venture to Australia to play international matches. Grace was so good he even treated rumours of his own decline with disdain. In 1895, aged 46 and weighing well over 20st, he became the first batsman to hit 1,000 runs in May and score 100 career hundreds.

Legend: Grace was truly the father of English cricket

Grace *factfile*

Born: 18.7.1848, Gloucestershire
Died: 23.10.1915
Country: England
Tests: 22 **Runs:** 1,098
Hundreds: 2 **Average:** 32.29

3

Jack Hobbs

Jack Hobbs was one of the finest batsmen ever to play the game – and he had the perfect initiation with a father who was groundsman at Jesus College, Cambridge. Perhaps because of this, Hobbs appeared to have total mastery of every pitch he played on.

He scored over 61,000 runs and 197 first-class hundreds, despite losing five years to World War One and the fact that by the time he was 40 years old he had scored only 99 of those centuries. In his 46th year, Hobbs scored an incredible 2,542 runs at an even more unlikely average – 82. From such a career, it is

PLAYER'S CIGARETTES

J. B. HOBBS (SURREY)

difficult to pick individual highlights. But against Australia in 1926 and 1929, he and Herbert Sutcliffe shared partnerships of 172 and 105 on venomous wickets to secure famous England victories. And in a county match for Surrey against Leicester in 1920, he scored 134 – which was more than the opposition could put together in both their innings. His greatest season was 1925 when he scored 16 hundreds, including one innings of 266 in a match between the Gentlemen and the Players. It was almost incidental that he was the first man to score 5,000 Test runs. His skill, allied to his unfailingly gentlemanly conduct on and off the pitch makes him a true cricketing great. He was knighted in 1953.

The Master: left, Hobbs testing a bat in 1922; above, in 1926, although aged well over 40 he was still at the height of his scoring career

Hobbs *factfile*

Born: 16.12.1882, Surrey
Died: 21.12.1963
Country: England
Tests: 61 **Runs:** 5410
Hundreds: 15 **Average:** 56.94

Gary Sobers

4

On the field, Gary Sobers could look languid to the point of uninterest. But the finest all-rounder the game has ever produced was capable of turning a match with a moment of unexpected genius. Not only was Sobers the best batsman of his era, he was a versatile left-arm bowler and a fielder without equal in any position. He is, of course, immortalised by the six sixes in one over that he hit for Nottinghamshire against Glamorgan in 1968 – but from his Test debut aged 18 against England in 1954, where he took 4-75, to his last, again against England, in 1974 where he became the first West Indian to take 100 wickets against England, Sobers dominated the game. His first Test century, in 1958, was part of a score of 365 not out against Pakistan; a record for Test matches. And even the great Don Bradman claimed that his 254 for the Rest of the World XI v Australia was 'one of the historic events in cricket'.

As a captain, Sobers was less successful. Under his often distracted leadership, the West Indies won only nine out of 39 Tests. That was all forgotten, however, in 1975 when he was knighted by the Queen.

Sobers *factfile*

With the Wisden Trophy he won in 1966

Born: 28.7.36, Barbados
Country: West Indies
Tests: 93 **Runs:** 8,032
Hundreds: 26 **Average:** 57.78

Bat and ball man: left, in 1973, near the end of his Test career Sobers was still an impressive force; right, at the Oval for the 5th Test between England and the West Indies, 1966 — the great left-handed all-rounder averaged over 100 in that series with the bat, and took 20 wickets too

I n just 50 glittering days in 1994, Brian Lara served notice that he was the best batsman in the world, and one of the most brilliant in cricketing history. First came 715 runs in just five Red Stripe Cup matches for Trinidad and Tobago, including 180 against Jamaica. England were the unfortunate tourists that year, and Lara duly caned them with 167 at Georgetown and a record-breaking 365 in the final Test at Antigua. English bowlers were then less than delighted to hear that Lara had signed for Warwickshire for the summer.

Their fears were realised as he proceeded to score centuries in each of his first five Championship matches, culminating in a massive 501 not out against Durham at Edgaston – 390 of which he scored in one day. Three weeks later, at Northampton, Lara scored 197 off just 195 balls against an attack which included Curtly Ambrose. He finished with the exceptional total of 1,551 runs, including seven hundreds in eight innings, and two records: the highest innings in both Test and first-class cricket, making him the first to hold both simultaneously since Bradman.

Unsurprisingly, Lara was unable to sustain such form. He had a petulant streak which at times was to the detriment of his own game and his appointment as West Indies' captain coincided with a disastrous slump in his country's fortunes. He remains, however, capable of breathtaking batting feats and it is only a matter of time before he proves once again that he is the best.

Brian Lara

lara *factfile*

Born: 2.5.69, Santa Cruz
Country: West Indies
Tests: 54
Runs: 4,550
Hundreds: 10
Average: 51.70

Clean sweep: Lara times another stroke to perfection, this time against the Aussies in 1998 at Sabina Park

As he traipsed off the field at Lord's after the second Ashes Test of 1981 with boos ringing in his ears and having scored a pair, Ian Botham's career was at its lowest ebb. It is typical of England's greatest modern all-rounder that such despair was to provide the springboard for some of his most astonishing feats.

Aided by Bob Willis, Botham, with 50 and 149 runs and 6-95, destroyed the Australians in the next Test at Headingley. At Edgbaston in the Fourth Test, he took five wickets for one run in 26

Here's the beef: unorthodox shots didn't stop Ian Botham making 139 in the Brisbane Test in 1986

Botham *factfile*

Born: 24.11.55, Cheshire
Country: England
Tests: 102 **Runs:** 5,200
Hundreds: 14 **Average:** 33.54
Wickets: 383 **Average:** 28.40

Ian Botham

balls to give England a 2-1 lead. And at Old Trafford, Botham provided what many believe was his greatest innings – 118 from 102 balls including six sixes and 13 fours to secure a famous series win. Botham had been marked out as special ever since his debut against Australia in 1977 when he took 5-74 at Trent Bridge. In Tests he scored 14 hundreds, took 383 wickets and held 120 catches – mostly of unbelievable quality. At first-class level, he was often unstoppable. In 1985, playing for Somerset against Northants at Weston-Super-Mare, Botham needed just two more sixes to equal Arthur Wellard's 1935 record of 66 sixes in a first-class season. Botham promptly hit eight sixes in a terrifying innings of 137 off 147 balls. Although later he put on weight and his run-up became more of a trundle, his reflexes stayed razor-sharp and his batting could revive fond memories of the great man at his prime.

Imperious: Richards sweeps during a century v India at Bombay in 1983. Right, pulling Botham outta sight at The Oval

Viv Richards

There was always a swagger about Viv Richards, an insouciance which almost dared the world's best bowlers to get him out. At his prime, such confidence was fully justified. Richards was a magnificent batsman, and to watch him was to witness a savage beauty in action. His innings of 291 against England at The Oval in 1976 was a major highlight in a career littered with them. It brought his total number of runs in Tests during that year to a record 1,710 at an average of 90 and established him as the best batsman in the world.

Like Len Hutton, Richards's Test career had started less than auspiciously – with 4 and 3 against India. Again like Hutton, Richards established himself immediately afterwards, with a commanding 192 not out. By 1985, he had scored 19 centuries in 77 Tests and was averaging 54 – and that does not include the Packer matches he played between 1977 and 1979 when he was at his peak, scoring four hundreds and averaging 86.20. With Ian Botham and Joel Garner, Richards formed a fearsome triumvirate which helped Somerset dominate county cricket in the mid-1980s. He was made captain of the West Indies in 1986, but this honour served mainly to mark a decline in his batting powers – although he could still turn it on when he so desired.

Always a great showman, he reserved his finest performances for Lord's. He scored 145 in his first Test there, and in eight one-day matches for West Indies and Somerset he finished on the winning side six times, including scores of 138 not out, 117 and 132 not out.

Richards *factfile*

Born: 7.3.52, Antigua
Died: 6.9.90
Country: West Indies
Tests: 121 **Runs:** 8,540
Hundreds: 24 **Average:** 50.23

Len Hutton

After a series defeat against India in 1951-52, English cricket was in an all too familiar position – crisis – when Yorkshire's Len Hutton was appointed the first professional captain since 1887. Although the move caused uproar among the establishment, in truth England could not have selected a better man. After an inauspicious start to his Test career (0 and 1 against New Zealand in 1937), Hutton scored a record 364 against Australia at the Oval in 1938. In 1939, he and Wally Hammond put on 264 in three hours against the West Indies. Hutton, despite a war injury which meant his left arm was two inches shorter than his right, resumed after the war as one of the finest opening batsmen in the world.

He was 36 when he was made England captain, and he repaid the selectors' faith in him by leading from the front with two centuries against India and a heroic 205 against the West Indies at Sabina Park.

As captain, Hutton lost only four out of 23 Tests. After his retirement, he was knighted for his services to the game.

8

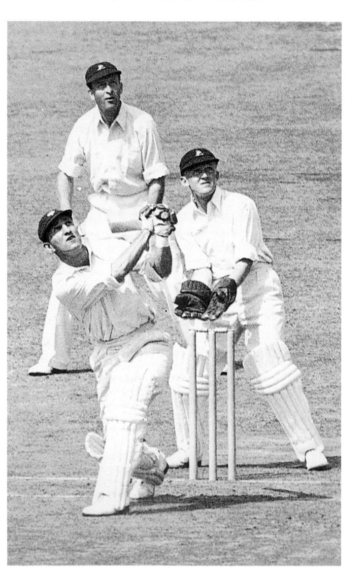

Yorkshire grit: Having one arm shorter than the other was no apparent handicap, at The Oval v South Africa in 1947, left. Right: Leaving the field after his record-breaking innings of 364 in 1938 – also at The Oval

Hutton *factfile*

Born: 23.6.16, Yorkshire
Died: 6.9.90
Country: England
Tests: 79 **Runs:** 6,971
Hundreds: 19 **Average:** 56.67

Shane Warne

9

Warne *factfile*

Born: 13.9.69, Melbourne

Country: Australia

Tests: 67

Wickets: 313

Average: 24.73

Shane Warne announced his arrival among the cricketing greats in the most dramatic style in the First Test against England at Old Trafford in 1993. Batsman Mike Gatting, generally regarded at the time as England's foremost master of spin, must have thought he was on for a few runs as the plump, peroxide-haired youngster's first delivery flew high and wide down the leg side. It was a ball that didn't even seem worth playing, and Gatting instead stuck out a pad just on the off-chance it would turn slightly as it landed. Turn it did – almost at 90 degrees – to clip the top of Gatting's off stump, leaving the batsman and everyone else in the ground utterly astonished by what has been dubbed The Ball of the Century. Apart from Warne himself, only the Australian skipper, Allan Border, knew what he was capable of. In the run-up to that Test, Border had taken care to keep his protégé under wraps. But even though the cat was now out of the bag, it did not stop Warne's extraordinary talent from making fools out of the world's top batsmen. Whether it was his leg-break,

Peroxide peril: Far left, Warne arrives in 1993 to blow Gatting away. Above: Nasser Hussain goes in Sydney, 1999, with a typical Warne celebration

his top spinner, his deadly 'flipper' or his googly, Warne had a repertoire that has made him one of the great – if not the greatest – spin bowlers of all time. In that 1993 series alone, he claimed 34 victims, including Graham Gooch's wicket five times. The following winter he was the leading wicket-taker against India and South Africa, and his hat-trick against England at Melbourne at the end of 1994 meant that he had taken 70 wickets in Tests for two years in succession. Injury has limited Warne's progress since then, but he remains one of cricket's most recognisable stars and, on his day, its most deadly bowler.

10

Wilfred Rhodes

Wilfred Rhodes's career lasted 30 years and in that time he transformed himself from a bowler who batted at 10 or 11, to the regular opening partner of Jack Hobbs. Between them, in 1911-12 in Melbourne, the pair put on the English record first-wicket partnership of 323. A left-handed bowler and right-handed batsman, Rhodes's figures are equally confusing. He took 31 wickets at 15.74 in Australia in 1903-04, yet eight years later he took no wickets but averaged 57.87 with the bat. At the age of 48, he was recalled for one last hurrah in the final Test of the 1926 Ashes. With 6-79, he helped England regain them.

Rhodes *factfile*

The last shall be first: From No 11 to opener was a remarkable journey. But even at the age of 48, right, he produced 6-79 for England and by 1930 he had taken 4,187 first-class wickets

Born: 29.10.1877, Yorkshire
Died: 8.7.1973
Country: England
Tests: 58 **Runs:** 2,325
Hundreds: 2 **Average:** 30.19

Batsman supreme Wally Hammond ruled the inter-war years and, in the 1930s, was the dominant force in English cricket. Tall and athletic, with a memorable off-drive, he proved almost impossible to winkle out once he had established himself at the crease. His 905 runs in the 1928-29 Ashes series was a record beaten only by Don Bradman, and his 336 not out in 318 minutes – including 10 sixes – in 1932-33 was a record score in Test cricket until 1938. That year, Hammond was made captain of England – although, as with so many other talented cricketers, he was not the best

WALTER HAMMOND

Off and away: Typical Hammond drive, left, against Australia in 1945

Wally Hammond

Hammond *factfile*

Born: 19.6.03, Kent
Died: 1.7.65
Country: England
Tests: 85 **Runs:** 7,249
Hundreds: 22 **Average:** 58.45

of skippers, being seen as aloof and unsympathetic to those who weren't as good as him. Not that there was *anyone* that good in England. He hit 240 in the 1938 Lord's Ashes Test and at The Oval declared at 930 for 7.

After the war, Hammond was still captain, but he was a shadow of the player he had been. He led England on the disastrous 1947 tour to Australia, where England lost the Ashes 3-0, and his final appearance was in a subsequent Test in Christchurch, New Zealand. Typically, he scored 79.

Sunil Gavaskar

A batsman from the textbook rather than one of natural ability, Sunil Gavaskar nevertheless rattled his way into the list of all-time greats with some extraordinary performances and figures. In all, he made a record 34 Test hundreds and scored over 10,000 runs at an average of 51.12. He particularly enjoyed playing against the West Indies. He made his Test debut there in 1970-71 and in just four matches plundered an astonishing 774 runs at an average of 151.80. During his 16-year Test career, he would make 13 centuries against the West Indies and eight against Australia.

Pulling power: Sunil hits Arnold for three in the Prudential Cup against England at Lord's in 1975

Gavaskar *factfile*

Born: 10.7.49, Bombay
Country: India
Tests: 125
Runs: 10122
Hundred: 34
Average: 51.12

13

'He plays very much the same as I played ... his compactness, his stroke production and technique.' Thus said the great Don Bradman – high praise indeed for the diminutive Sachin Tendulkar, who played his first Test match aged just 16 and has thrilled the world with his batting style ever since, becoming India's greatest superstar.

Ironically, he came to the game late. Born in Bombay, he was 10 when he first decided he wanted to play cricket. From that moment, there was no stopping him: Sachin practised eight hours a day, and on his first appearance for Bombay, aged 15, he scored an unbeaten hundred. That first Test, against Pakistan, was the following year. Against England, he scored a defiant 119 not out, becoming the second-youngest player to score a Test hundred. In 1996, he was made captain of India, but found the pressure too much and gave it up a year later. This only made him a more dangerous player, and in the following 18 months Tendulkar scored 14 Test hundreds.

Tiny terror: Only the captaincy temporarily stemmed the flow of centuries from Sachin Tendulkar's bat

Sachin Tendulkar

Tendulkar *factfile*

Born: 24.4.73, Bombay
Country: India
Tests: 61
Runs: 4,552
Hundreds: 16
Average: 54.84

Dennis Lillee

In December 1971, 21-year-old Dennis Lillee introduced himself to the world of cricket in spectacular fashion in Perth when he single-handedly destroyed a World XI, led by Gary Sobers, by taking 8-29 in 57 balls, the last six wickets for no run. With his tearaway style and lightning fast delivery, it was always only a matter of time before he was discovered. For much of the 1970s Lillee, with his trademark moustache and long black hair streaming behind him, was at the forefront of a devastating Australian pace attack alongside Jeff Thomson. On his first tour to England in 1972 he took 31 Test wickets at 17.76, skittling out a bemused home side and helping to square the series. His no-holds-barred style on that tour was to cause him career-threatening back problems, however. After an operation on his vertebrae, it was doubtful he would play again. Yet, with typical doggedness, Lillee fought his way back to fitness and replaced what he lost in pace with technical mastery of swing and movement off the pitch. In 1974-75, he and Thommo destroyed Mike Denness's England side. In just 70 Tests he took 355 wickets — and would have taken far more had he not decided to join Kerry Packer in the late 1970s.

Lillee *factfile*

Born: 18.7.49, Western Australia
Country: Australia
Tests: 70
Wickets: 355
Average: 23.92

Pace with purpose: Lillee in 1981, after he changed his action to save his back

Richards *factfile*

Born: 21.7.45, Natal
Country: South Africa
Tests: 4 **Runs:** 508
Hundreds: 2 **Average:** 72.57

Perfection: Richards beat the best in
his all-too-brief international career

Barry Richards

It was unfortunate that South Africa's lengthy ban from international sport meant Barry Richards would make only four Test appearances, for he was without doubt one of the world's most gifted batsmen. "He appears not to move at all, yet his feet twinkle," noted England skipper Colin Cowdrey. He did get his chance on the international stage, however, in the 1970s when he joined up with Kerry Packer. His performances against the likes of Dennis Lillee made the rest of the world's bowlers relieved that he was banned from the official stage.

With Hampshire, his county side from 1968, he once scored 96 and 69 in brilliant fashion against Australia's Jeff Thomson, and during one season with South Australia he averaged 109.85 and scored 325 runs in a day against Lillee. He excelled in his one and only Test series against Australia in 1969-70, scoring two centuries, averaging 72.57 and helping South Africa to a 4-0 series win. "It was hard to imagine how another mortal could approach such perfection," said his fellow countryman Mike Procter of the brilliant century which Richards completed just after lunch on the first day of the Durban Test.

S.F. Barnes

Remarkably for a bowler who is generally regarded as the best of them all, S.F. Barnes played only 27 Tests and two full seasons of first-class cricket for Lancashire, preferring instead to play in the Staffordshire league. Yet his 46-year career reached heights that will never again be attained. In all competitive matches, he claimed 6,229 wickets at 8.33 apiece. He took all 10 wickets in an innings 12 times, and in those 27 Tests he claimed 189 wickets at 16.43 and every 41.65 balls, an average and a strike rate unequalled by any 20th-century bowler. In just four matches in South Africa in 1913 he took 49 wickets, and his 34 wickets in the 1911-12 Ashes series not only gave England victory, but was an Ashes record for 13 years.

16

Barnes *factfile*

Born: 19.4.1873, Staffordshire
Died: 26.12.1967
Country: England
Tests: 27
Wickets: 189
Average: 16.43

Michael Holding

Geoffrey Boycott would willingly testify to the terrifying pace of Michael Holding who, with Andy Roberts and Malcolm Marshall, destroyed batting line-ups in the 1970s and '80s. At Bridgetown in 1981, Boycott faced what is regarded as the most hostile over ever. Ball one reared up and Boycott could only just glove it away from his face. He managed to flick his head away at the last moment from ball two. Ball three thumped painfully into his left thigh. Four, short and vicious, was fended to gully. Five shot with the noise of an angry wasp past Boycott's right ear. Six uprooted his off stump and sent it cartwheeling twenty yards towards the wicket-keeper.

Over and out: Holding gets his man, Boycott, with the last ball of the 'Over of the Century'

Holding *factfile*

Born: 16.2.54, Jamaica
Country: West Indies
Tests: 60
Wickets: 249
Average: 23.68

Imran Khan

A fine fast bowler and batsman, Imran's greatest achievement was as captain of Pakistan. Under his inspiring, not to say regal, leadership, a collection of often disparate and headstrong players were blended into a winning team that became a force in world cricket. It was Imran who led Pakistan to a famous victory in the 1992 World Cup in Australia and New Zealand and set them on the route to becoming one of the truly great one-day sides. This is not to decry his often brilliant feats with the ball. In the Test series against India in 1982-83 he took 40 wickets at 13.95. It was always clear, however, that Imran was looking at the bigger picture. After the 1992 triumph he retired from cricket in order to build a cancer hospital in Lahore. He has since entered the world of Pakistani politics and could even become his country's leader.

18

Imran *factfile*

Born: 25.11.52, Lahore
Country: Pakistan
Tests: 88 **Runs:** 3,807
Hundreds: 6
Average: 37.69
Wickets: 362
Average: 22.81

All-round inspiration: Imran's captaincy was the deciding factor in Pakistan's one-day success

Denis Compton

*D*enis Compton was not a classical batsman by any means. Indeed, as an FA Cup-winning wing for Arsenal, he was unlike most cricketers. He played with a gloriously improvised style and verve, and in the post-war years his matinée idol looks ensured him a huge following. Compton's peak was in 1947, when he provided a golden summer of batting brilliance against South Africa. He scored centuries in all four Tests: 163 at Trent Bridge, 115 at Old Trafford and 113 at The Oval. But he saved his best for the Second Test at Lord's, where he struck a majestic 208, shared a then record third-wicket stand of 370 with Bill Edrich and helped England to a crushing 10-wicket victory. In that series Compton scored a remarkable 753 runs. In all first-class games, he scored 18 centuries and smashed 3,816 runs. Eventually, his dual sporting life would catch up with him and he retired with a knee injury. Until his death in 1997 he kept his kneecap in a little box to remind him of a wonderful career.

19

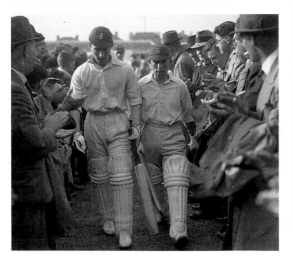

Everyone for Denis: The dashing and popular Compton (far left) with Bill Edrich in 1938. Later they would set a third-wicket record. Above: Taking the game to Pakistan at The Oval in 1954

Bill O'Reilly

Born: 23.5.18, Middlesex
Died: 23.4.97
Country: England
Tests: 78 **Runs:** 5,807
Hundreds: 17 **Average:** 50.06

PLAYER'S CIGARETTES

D. C. S. COMPTON

The records show that for most of his Test career – between 1932 and 1946, with an interruption for World War Two – Bill O'Reilly was the best bowler in the world. His use of the leg-break was devastating, a fact recognised by his team-mate and occasional sparring partner Don Bradman, who called him the best he had ever faced or seen.

Of Irish stock, Aussie O'Reilly hated batsmen with a passion. "Hitting Bill O'Reilly for four was like disturbing a hive of bees," said Bradman. In his seven years at the top, O'Reilly took 144 wickets in only 27 Tests.

In the Bodyline series of 1932, it is often forgotten that he was instrumental in Australia's only win, when he took 10-129 from 59 overs. In 1934, he offered perhaps his best Test performance when at Headingley in the final match he took 10-122 and helped to retain the Ashes.

Net gain: Bradman called him the best

O'Reilly *factfile*

Born: 20.12.05, New South Wales
Died: 6.10.92
Country: Australia
Tests: 27
Wickets: 144
Average: 22.59

20

(21)

Sutcliffe *factfile*

Born: 24.11.1894, Yorkshire
Died: 22.1.78
Country: England
Tests: 54
Runs: 4555
Hundreds: 16
Average: 60.73

The immortal opening duo of Hobbs (far left) and Sutcliffe come out to bat for England against Australia at Leeds in 1926. They were renowned for their running together and their ability to 'grind out' a partnership

Herbert Sutcliffe

Alongside Jack Hobbs, Herbert Sutcliffe formed a well-nigh waterproof opening partnership for England. In their 25 Tests together, they made over 100 14 times and their average first-wicket partnership was 88. Unlike Hobbs, Sutcliffe was not a natural talent. Instead, he worked hard at ensuring his technique was perfect. He particularly enjoyed playing against Australia, where his average was 66.85. But he set about getting runs in his own unflappable manner against any opposition, scoring 149 first class centuries and, in 1931, scoring at an average of 96.96.

Arthur Shrewsbury

A cricketing pioneer, Arthur Shrewsbury was one of the small group of English players who took the game to Australia at the end of the last century. And of the seven Tests he captained England there between 1881 and 1888, he won five. Alongside his great rival W.G. Grace, Shrewsbury was one of the game's major record holders: the first England captain to score 100, the highest individual score against Australia (164) and the first to make 1,000 runs.

Shrewsbury *factfile*

Born: 11.4.1856, Nottinghamshire
Died: 19.5.1903
Country: England
Tests: 23 **Runs:** 1277
Hundreds: 3 **Average:** 35.47

Arthur Shrewsbury: The first England captain to score a Test century

22

Headley hits a boundary against England in 1939, when he became the first man to score a century in each innings at Lord's

George Headley

Headley *factfile*

Born: 30.5.09, Jamaica
Died: 30.11.83
Country: West Indies
Tests: 22 **Runs:** 2190
Hundreds: 10 **Average:** 60.83

George Headley was known as the 'Black Bradman', and with good reason. In style and prolific run-scoring, he came close to emulating the extraordinary Australian. In the pre-war era, Headley dominated every bowler he came across. In 1928 he scored 71 and 211 for Jamaica against the MCC, and in his first Test series for the West Indies against England in 1930 he hit 176, 114, 112, and 233. Indeed in just 19 Test matches up until 1939, Headley scored 10 hundreds and had an average of 66.72.

Had war not intervened when he was at his prime, he might even have gone on to eclipse Bradman. In the event, when he next played Test cricket, Headley was nearly 40 and, sadly, was not a patch on the great batsman he had once been.

Richie Benaud

He now commands respect as one of the foremost cricket commentators, but in his playing career Richie Benaud was equally revered. A wrist spinner of often devastating accuracy, Benaud was also a fine batsman and fielder. It was as a daring and knowledgeable captain of Australia that he will be best remembered, however. After making his Test debut against the West Indies in 1951-52, he became captain for the 1958-59 Ashes series against Peter May's England. Australia took the series 4-0, with Benaud's contribution as an all-rounder and skipper immense. Impressive victories in Pakistan and India were followed by a riveting series against the West Indies which Australia won.

Benaud's moment of glory came against England in 1961. With the sides level, Benaud took 5-12 to win the match and the series. In 1963-64 against South Africa, he became the first Australian to score 2000 runs and take 200 wickets in Test cricket. Of the six Test series in which he led Australia, five were won and the other drawn.

Benaud *factfile*

24

Born: 6.10.30, New South Wales
Country: Australia
Tests: 63 **Wickets:** 248
Average: 27.03

Worthy of comment: Richie Benaud spins Australia to an Ashes Test victory at Old Trafford in 1961

Kapil Dev

Kapil Dev is the greatest all-round cricketer India has ever produced. It took him just 25 Tests, aged 21 years 27 days, to complete 1000 runs and 100 wickets – the youngest player to complete the 'double' in Test cricket.

His career was peppered with spectacular moments, many of them reserved for matches against England at Lord's. In 1982, in a single evening, he battered 89 in 55 minutes and then took three England wickets in his first four overs. In 1990, with India nine wickets down and still requiring 24 to avoid the follow on, he dispatched Eddie Hemmings for four consecutive sixes. Although he became India's captain and led them to victory in the 1983 World Cup, Kapil's reputation was not made as a great tactician. His leadership powers were based solely on his swashbuckling style, which puts him up there with that other great all-rounder of the time, Ian Botham.

25

Kapil Dev *factfile*

Born: 6.1.59, Chandigarh
Country: India
Tests: 131
Runs: 5248
Hundreds: 8
Average: 31.05
Wickets: 434
Average: 29.64

Kapil Dev treats the crowd to a typical show of skill against the West Indies in the Nehru Cup in 1989

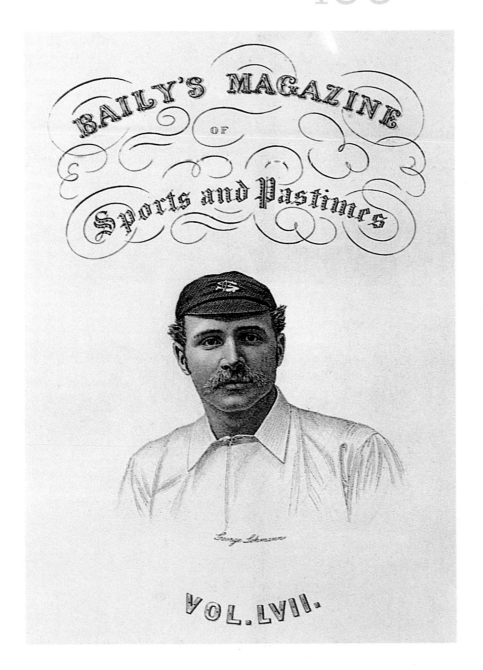

George Lohmann

Lohmann was the Ian Botham of his day, a magnificent cricketer who became a household name at the end of the last century. His career, however, was tragically cut short by tuberculosis at the age of just 36. A medium-pacer, Lohmann's ability lay in being able to vary his deliveries to the extent that opposing batsmen were left totally bamboozled. In 1886, he took 12 Australian wickets in a match at The Oval while in his first three Tests in Australia later that year, he took 25 wickets for 189 runs. Lohmann's fitness and physique enabled him to get through a tremendous amount of bowling. For Surrey, he took 1,458 wickets – a strike rate of nearly eight a match. His England striking rate of 6.2 a match has only been bettered by the great S.F. Barnes.

26

Lohmann *factfile*

Born: 2.6.1865, Surrey
Died: 1.12.1901
Country: England
Tests: 18
Wickets: 112
Average: 10.75

Alan Knott

lan Knott was not simply a brilliant wicketkeeper, his five Test hundreds puts him in the category of one of England's finest all-rounders. Superbly fit and agile, he made the England team at the age of 21 – young for a keeper – and played 95 Tests. He would have played many more had he not signed for Kerry Packer as well as the rebel South African tour led by Graham Gooch. It was in tandem with his Kent colleague, spinner Derek Underwood, that Knott took many of his 269 Test victims.

Knott in action: Alan Knott claims another hapless victim behind the stumps in 1970

Knott *factfile*

Born: 9.4.46, Kent **Country:** England
Tests: 95 **Runs:** 4389
Hundreds: 5 **Average:** 32.75
Catches: 1211 **Stumpings:** 133

Steve Waugh

It is testament to his dogged determination to succeed that when Mark Taylor decided to call it a day as Australian captain, his obvious replacement was Steve Waugh. Now regarded as one of the most consistent Test performers in the world, Waugh has had to work hard at his game. One of two brothers currently dominating cricket in Australia, Steve has never had the natural ability of twin Mark. Instead, he has displayed an unrivalled temperament and inner strength. Moreover, he has proved an invaluable matchwinner on many occasions. In 14 Test series between 1993 and 1997, he topped Australia's averages eight times. His finest performances came during the tour to the Caribbean in 1994-95, in which the Aussies won a series against the West Indies for the first time in 15 years. Against hostile bowling, he scored 50s in the first three Tests and a magnificent 200 in the fourth and deciding Test in Jamaica. Here, he stayed at the crease for 10 hours, faced more than 150 short-pitched deliveries, ended up black and blue, but doggedly broke the back of the West Indies' bowlers to clinch victory for his side.

Steve declares Waugh on another English bowler in 1989

Steve Waugh *factfile*

Born: 2.6.65, New South Wales
Country: Australia
Tests: 103
Runs: 6480
Hundreds: 14
Average: 48.72

28

Frederick Spofforth

29

When he arrived on his first tour of England in 1878, Frederick Spofforth stunned both crowds and opposition. Quite simply, they'd never seen anything quite like his bowling action, which consisted of a nine-pace run-up, a huge leap in the air and a devastatingly quick delivery. It earned him the nickname 'The Demon', and it's a fair assumption most of his 94 Test victims were scared out of their crease. Spofforth was also phenomenally accurate, aiming wherever possible at the stumps with yorkers and cutters. Against a strong MCC side at Lord's in 1878, Spofforth took 6-4 – including a hat-trick – in the first innings with just 23 balls, and 4-36 in 36 balls in the second. Seven of his wickets were bowled, two stumped and one caught-and-bowled, including W.G. Grace for a second-ball duck. The MCC were dumped for 33 and 19 and beaten in a day. Spofforth was also instrumental in Australia's first, historic win against England at The Oval in 1891, with a match-winning

Frederick Spofforth was the first in a long line of Australian demon bowlers

Spofforth *factfile*

Born: 9.9.1853, New South Wales
Died: 4.6.1926
Country: Australia
Tests: 18
Wickets: 94
Average: 18.41

spell of 4-2 from 11 overs. His duels with Grace left the great man in no doubt that Spofforth was the best bowler in the world.

Spofforth himself readily agreed: "I never had any particular difficulty getting him (Grace) out," he boasted. "I clean bowled him seven times."

Graham Gooch

All the threes: Gooch on his way to 333, above, against India at Lord's, 1990 and, left, in the twilight of his career in 1994

So often it seemed that as all around him collapsed into disarray, the four-square figure of Graham Gooch stood rock-like to save the day for England. At Headingley against the West Indies in the First Test of 1991, his innings of 154 not out was his finest, a masterclass of dogged determination and technique in the face of dwindling odds which won the match. But there were other highlights in a distinguished Test career which began, ironically, with a pair against Australia in 1975, and reached fruition when he was into his forties. As captain of his country, he averaged 60 with the bat. In 1990, in the Lord's Test against India, he scored 333 in the first innings and 123 in the second – the first batsman to complete such a feat.

Gooch *factfile*

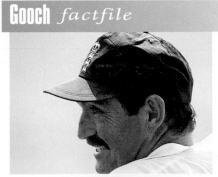

Born: 23.7.53, Essex **Country:** England
Tests: 118 **Runs:** 8900 **Hundreds:** 20
Average: 42.58

31

Godfrey Evans

un to watch, yet brilliant at his art, Godfrey Evans was the precursor to another entertaining Kent and England wicket-keeper, Alan Knott. Evans possessed cat-like reflexes which often had a batsman stumped so quickly, he didn't realise it until he saw the bails on the ground. In 1954-55, he helped Len Hutton's side to Ashes victory with spectacular catches off the bowling of Frank Tyson as well as hitting the winning run in the Fourth Test. Like Knott, he could also bat. Against India at Lord's in 1952, Evans scored 104 – 98 of them before lunch on the third day.

Above: Evans stumps Rae of the West Indies at Trent Bridge

Evans *factfile*

Born: 18.8.20, Kent
Country: England
Tests: 91 **Runs:** 2439
Hundreds: 2 **Average:** 20.49
Catches: 173 **Stumpings:** 46

Victor Trumper

For once, statistics are no measure of how good a batsman was. Victor Trumper was not prolific like Bradman, he was simply the best batsman of his time. Indeed there are some who believe him to have been better than Bradman. There was no delivery, short or long, that he would not attack. Bowlers would appeal for lbw, only to see him whip the ball away at the last second. In the wet English summer of 1902, Trumper scored 11 centuries. In 1913-14, he hit 293 in just 180 minutes against New Zealand. He was sporadic, yet brilliant. Only his performances in grade cricket in Australia give the modern cricket fan an idea of how good he was: in 19 seasons, he scored 8,946 runs at 69.34. When he died aged just 37 from Bright's Disease in 1915, the cricketing world had lost a true star.

32

Trumper *factfile*

Born: 2.11.1877, New South Wales
Died: 28./.1915
Country: Australia
Tests: 48
Runs: 3163
Hundreds: 31
Average: 39.04

Mike Procter

Procter *factfile*

Born: 15.9.46, Natal
Country: South Africa **Tests:** 7
Wickets: 41 **Average:** 15.02

Like Barry Richards, Mike Procter's chance at a place on the world stage was ruined by South Africa's ban. The seven Tests he did play before his country was banished – all against Australia in 1967 – were enough to reveal an all-rounder of rare talent. He took 41 wickets at 15.02 and scored 226 runs. A fearsomely fast bowler who also scored six consecutive centuries for Rhodesia in the 1970-71 Currie Cup, Procter instead gave his lot to a thankful Gloucestershire for nearly 20 years.

The 21,000 runs and 1,400 wickets he amassed for his county are testament to his astonishing ability, and the besotted West Country cricket fans changed the name of the county to Proctershire in his honour.

All-round superstar: Procter, above, on his way to a century for Gloucestershire during the 1973 Gillette Cup semi-final

Clive Lloyd

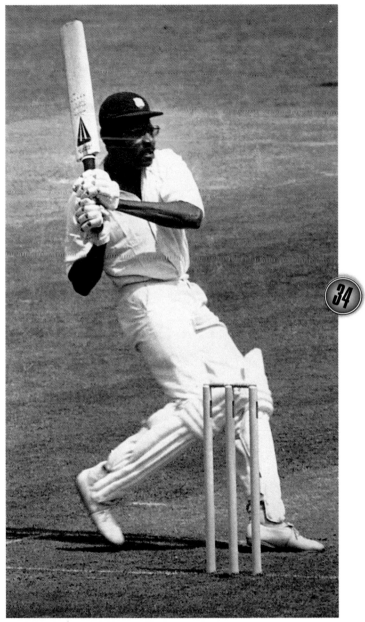

34

For a man who appeared at first sight to be gangling and uncoordinated, Clive Lloyd moved like a cat both at the crease and in the field. As a captain, his tactical awareness, approachability and ability to adapt (by using four fast bowlers) made him one of the most successful ever to hold the office. Indeed it is easy to forget that before he was made captain in 1974-75, Lloyd was already established as an exceptional batsman. He scored 82 and 78 not out on his debut against India in 1966, and against England in 1968 he scored centuries in the first and third Tests. His finest form, however – 163 and 242 in a series against India – coincided with the beginning of his highly successful reign as captain. He led for 74 matches, in which he won 14 out of 18 series as well as the World Cups of 1975 – when he scored 102 off 82 balls in the Final against Australia – and 1979.

Sweet revenge: Lloyd and Holding celebrate at The Oval in 1976, having won the series in which England captain Tony Greig had planned to make them "grovel". **Right:** Lloyd's greatest innings, in the 1975 World Cup Final at Lord's

Lloyd *factfile*

Born: 31.8.44, British Guyana
Country: West Indies
Tests: 110 **Runs:** 7515
Hundreds: 19 **Average:** 46.67

Curtly Ambrose

Curtly Elconn Lynwall Ambrose came from tiny Swetes Village in Antigua, but went on to bestride the world of fast bowling as a 6ft 7in colossus. His speed was terrifying, but what set him apart was his devastating accuracy, which has been considered better than that of Ray Lindwall or Harold Larwood.

Like Brian Lara, he made his first impact in inter-island cricket, taking a record 35 wickets at 15.51. Against England in 1990, his unforgettable spell with the new ball in the final session of the Fourth Test in Bridgetown turned the series the West Indies' way. Ambrose took five wickets in five overs for innings figures of 8-45. In the final Test, he won the match with a haul of six wickets. From that moment, brilliant figures kept coming, with perhaps his best being 8-81, 10-120 and 9-79 in the series against South Africa in 1994. His Test record of 337 wickets from 80 matches at 21.16 speaks for itself.

Curtly Ambrose – a quiet man, except when appealing for a batsman's scalp

Ambrose *factfile*

Born: 21.10.63, Antigua
Country: West Indies
Tests: 80
Wickets: 337
Average: 21.16

Graeme Pollock

Graeme Pollock was averaging over 60 from 23 Tests with the bat when the plug was pulled on his Test career by South Africa's expulsion from world cricket. Who knows what he might have ended up with, for Pollock was a supreme left-handed batsman even as a youngster.

He made his maiden first-class century aged just 16, and three years later, still only 19, he scored 122 and 175 in the 1963-64 Test series against Australia. England's bowlers suffered no respite either. In 1964, Pollock helped South Africa to their first series win in England with 125 at Trent Bridge.

He signed off from international cricket in fine style with 274 against Australia in Durban in 1969-70. The Pollock name is not forgotten in world cricket, however: Graeme's son Shaun has developed into a formidable Test all-rounder.

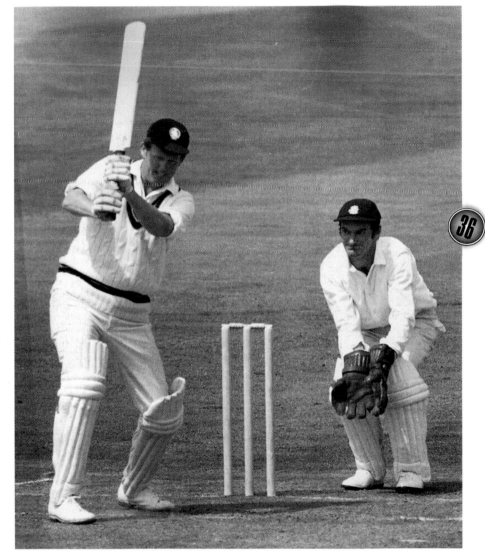

36

Graeme Pollock *factfile*

Born: 27.2.44, Western Province
Country: South Africa
Tests: 23
Runs: 2256
Hundreds: 7
Average: 60.97

Steamroller: Allan Knott watches as Graeme Pollock makes his mark with a century against England during the Rest of the World series of 1970

Greg Chappell

Best-known these days for leading the bulk of Australia's best players into Kerry Packer's cricket circus, Greg Chappell was, in fact, an elegant batsman and a highly successful Australian captain. Very different to his elder brother Ian in appearance and style, he made his Test debut against England in 1970 and scored a century. Under his brother's captaincy, he continued to punish England with centuries in the 1972 Ashes – creating history at The Oval when he and Ian became the first brothers to score hundreds in the same innings of a Test. Having been groomed by Ian, Greg took over the Australian captaincy against the West Indies in 1975-76 and led his side to a 5-1 victory. Everything unravelled in 1977, however, when, following a heavy defeat by England, Chappell defected to Packer and remained in the wilderness for two years. Upon his return he was immediately made captain against England.

There was a tungsten streak running through the Chappell brothers and Greg was no exception. In a one-day international against New Zealand in 1981, he ordered his brother Trevor to bowl the last ball of the match underarm to prevent New Zealand hitting the six they needed for victory. The acrimony this caused did little to sweeten Greg Chappell's already soured public image.

37

Chappell *factfile*

Born: 7.8.48, South Australia
Country: Australia
Tests: 87
Runs: 7110
Hundreds: 24
Average: 53.86

Greg Chappell hits four during his innings of 114 during the third Ashes test at Melbourne in February 1980

Richard Hadlee

Hard graft made Richard Hadlee into one of the great bowlers. Every step of his career was carefully plotted and paced. Hadlee knew precisely what was required to reach the top, and he shrewdly watched other great bowlers to learn where to go right and where not to go wrong. He learned all the time, so that in his mid-thirties, he was deadlier than he was when he was 10 years younger. Accurate and pacy, Hadlee accumulated 431 Test wickets, at an astonishing average of five a match. This was a world record until he was overhauled by the great Kapil Dev.

Hadlee *factfile*

Richard Hadlee is undoubtedly New Zealand's best ever cricketer and, indeed, one of the greatest bowlers of all time. He enjoyed playing against England more than anyone else, taking 97 wickets against them in 21 Test matches. He is seen, left, appealing for another English wicket at Edgbaston in 1990 – the year in which he was knighted

Born: 3.7.51, Canterbury
Country: New Zealand
Tests: 86 **Wickets:** 431
Average: 22.29

38

Frank Worrell

39

The first black man to be appointed captain for more than one match, Frank Worrell at the age of 36 was largely responsible for uniting the West Indies into a team rather than a collection of

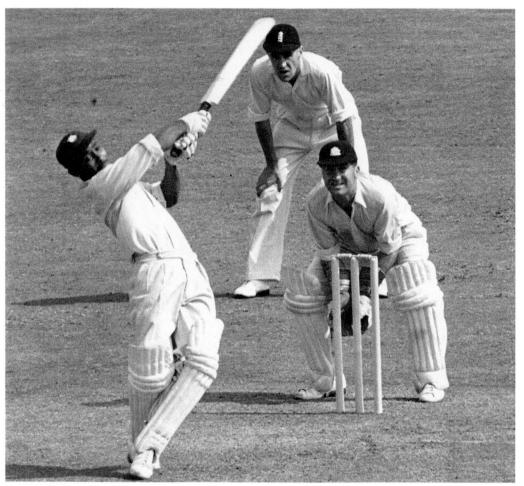

Wicketkeeper Godfrey Evans can only watch as Frank Worrell hits a match-winning 261 at Trent Bridge in 1950

Worrell *factfile*

Born: 1.8.24, Barbados
Died: 13.3.67
Country: West Indies
Tests: 51 **Runs:** 3860
Hundreds: 9 **Average:** 49.48

talented individuals from rival islands. A natural ambassador, he combined leadership with consummate ability, scoring nine hundreds and 3860 runs during his 51-Test career. In his first seven Tests he scored 833 runs at an average of 104.12. His first series, in Australia in 1960-61, was a triumph of excitement and skill – even though the West Indies lost the series. Under Worrell they won the next two. At the end of the 1963 series in England, he retired, his job done. After his tragic death two years later from leukaemia, Worrell was honoured and remembered in a service at Westminster Abbey, the first time that a sportsman had been so recognised.

Nuggety Aussie Rod Marsh first served notice as a batsman when, on his first-class debut, he scored 104 off the bowling of Hall and Griffith. But it was as a brooding, bitching, cajoling, haranguing presence behind the stumps that he attained legendary status. With Lillee and Thomson haring in, and Marsh giving the verbals from wicketkeeper, it was no fun being a batsman against the Australians in the 1970s. Beneath the bluster, Marsh was also a supreme keeper and athlete. Besides taking the most dismissals in a series (28) against England in 1982-83 and becoming the first Australian keeper to score a Test century, he claimed a record 355 victims – 95 of them off the bowling of Dennis Lillee.

Marsh mellow: Rodney Marsh was anything but mellow behind the stumps but no one can deny that this vociferous Aussie was one of the best wicketkeepers ever. He was also at home with the bat, racking up an average of 26.52 in his 96-Test areer

Marsh *factfile*

Born: 11.11.47, Western Australia
Country: Australia
Tests: 96
Runs: 3633
Hundreds: 3
Average: 26.51
Catches: 343
Stumpings: 12

Rodney Marsh

No less a batsman than England's great Len Hutton regarded Ray Lindwall as the finest bowler he ever faced, and duels between the pair were a highlight of Ashes matches in the post-war years. In tandem with Keith Miller, Lindwall formed a devastating two-pronged attack that was the precursor of the Lillee-Thomson axis in the 1970s. Lindwall was able to swing the ball in both directions, and often too late for the batsman to readjust in time. An all-round sportsman and natural athlete, Lindwall was also no mean competitor with the bat, scoring Test hundreds against England and the West Indies.

41

Lindwall in action at The Oval in 1953

Lindwall *factfile*

Born: 3.10.21, New South Wales
Country: Australia
Tests: 61 **Wickets:** 228
Average: 23.03

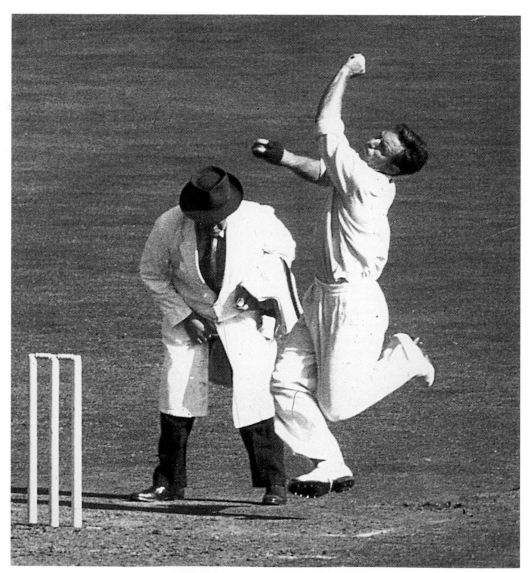

Ray Lindwall

Fred Trueman

Fired by a passionate ambition and a gritty Yorkshire determination, Fred Trueman set out to become the best bowler in the world. He succeeded, eventually. But in getting to the pinnacle, he also became one of cricket's most enduring characters. With his no-nonsense approach to the game, his innate hatred of its establishment figures, and his snorting, powerhouse delivery, he won the nickname 'Fiery Fred' and the hearts of the public. His yorker was deadly, as was his slower paced off cutter. Trueman delighted in intimidating batsmen – especially those from Oxbridge. "Ah'll pin thee t' sightscreen!" he would rumble. His figures speak for themselves: the first bowler to take 300 Test wickets, the highest ever aggregate of first-class wickets (2,304) and a strike rate of one wicket every 49 balls. At Headingley in 1961, he destroyed Australia with five-wicket bursts in two innings and at Edgbaston in 1963 he skittled the West Indies with a spell of six wickets for 24 balls.

42

Trueman *factfile*

Born: 6.2.31, Yorkshire
Country: England
Tests: 67
Wickets: 307
Average: 21.57

The Trueman Show: Fred warms up at Headingley in 1953

Jim Laker

According to his England team-mate Trevor Bailey, big Jim Laker was "the finest off-spinner I have ever seen and, probably, in the entire history of the game". At 6ft, with a model action and a prodigious ability to spin the ball, this was undoubtedly true of the Yorkshire-born bowler at the end of his career. Yet, ironically, Laker was initially viewed with suspicion by the selectors, especially after his bowling was destroyed by the Australians at Headingley in 1948. Between 1948 and 1956, he played in just 24 Tests and was passed over for 50 more – despite the fact that he played series-deciding roles at The Oval in 1951, '53 and '55 and got hat-tricks four times. The Ashes series in 1956, however, was to be his annus mirabilis at the age of 34. He claimed 46 wickets – an Ashes record – for an average of just 9.60 in the five Tests. In the Fourth Test in Manchester, he recorded his historic figures of 19-90

43

– 9-37 in the first innings and 10-53 in the second. This astonishing feat remains probably the most famous record in the history of cricket.

Jim Laker in action for Surrey against Australia shortly before his 19-wicket haul

Laker *factfile*

Born: 9.2.22, Yorkshire
Died: 23.4.86
Country: England
Tests: 46 **Wickets:** 193
Average: 21.24

David Gower

Undoubtedly the most graceful England batsman on the pitch, and debonair off it, David Gower at times hit the very heights of batting brilliance without ever being able to prevent slumps into the very depths. On his Test debut against Pakistan in 1978, the left-hander hit the ball for four – and so began a collection of runs bettered only by Geoffrey Boycott and Graham Gooch. Against Australia he scored an innings of 215, he got 200 against India and 173 against Pakistan. There were those who thought he had the natural ability to captain his country, but it was as skipper that his triumphs and disasters were most keenly felt.

His first full series as captain was at home to the West Indies in 1984-5, which ended in the first ever 5-0 whitewash in England. Yet the following tour to India was won, not least because of Gower's calm leadership in the face of political upheaval following the assassination of Indira Ghandi. In 1985 he won the Ashes, but was slammed following another 5-0 drubbing by the West Indies. Other than his batting, Gower did little to endear himself to the selectors. He once buzzed a match in a biplane, and was often seen to be so laid-back as to be horizontal. Still, it is his languid, often beautiful batting style by which he will be rightly remembered.

Gower *factfile*

Born: 1.4.57, Kent
Country: England
Tests: 117
Runs: 8231
Hundreds: 18
Average: 44.25

Gower celebrates with Mike Gatting – a future successor as England captain – as he leads his country to victory in India in 1985

44

Geoffrey Boycott

Infuriating, obstinate, opinionated – but how England could do with an opening batsman who could hang around as long as Geoffrey Boycott these days. At times, watching Boycott at the crease was akin to pulling teeth, yet his record speaks for itself: of the 112 batsmen to have made more than 25,000 first-class runs, only Don Bradman (95.14) has a better career average than Boycott (56.83). He announced himself in 1965 with a brilliant century in the 1965 Gillette Cup Final, but thereon in, his career became clouded with controversy. He seemed to be constantly at war with the management and players at Yorkshire and, when passed over for the England captaincy, he made himself unavailable for Test matches from 1974 until 1977.

Typically, on his return to the England side, he scored his hundredth 100 in front of his adoring fans at Headingley.

45

Boycott *factfile*

Born: 21.10.40, Yorkshire
Country: England
Tests: 108
Runs: 8114
Hundreds: 22
Average: 47.72

The perfectionist: Boycott did not often set the stage alight, but he held it for longer than any of his contemporaries

C.B. Fry

Charles Burgess Fry was a brilliant cricketer – but then, he was brilliant at whatever sport he turned his hand to. He held the world long-jump record for 21 years, played football for England and rugby for the Barbarians, yet still found time to amass almost 40,000 runs at an average of 50.22. With his Greek god looks, Fry was almost too good to be true. In 1901, his last six innings of the season were all centuries. His next innings in April 1902 saw him chalk up 82 for London County v Surrey – an innings made all the more remarkable by the fact that he had played for Southampton in the FA Cup Final two days earlier. He once said of his prodigious batting: "I really only had one stroke, but it went to 10 different parts of the field." He was more succinctly summed up by one contemporary observer who wrote: "In cricket, triumph and disaster will come again; but in this world, Charles Fry will not."

C.B. Fry *factfile*

Born: 25.4.1872, Sussex
Died: 7.9.56
Country: England **Tests:** 26
Runs: 1223 **Hundreds:** 2
Average: 32.18

Jack of all trades, master of all: C.B. Fry was a truly great sporting all-rounder who was in his prime at the turn of the century

46

Brian Statham

I n 1955, Brian Statham's fast-bowling partnership with Frank Tyson blew away the Australians and helped Len Hutton's side regain the Ashes. It was a devastating pairing repeated 20 years later when Lillee and Thomson returned the compliment. Tyson took 28 wickets to Statham's 18, but it was Statham's unerring accuracy and stamina which allowed the pacier Tyson to thrive. First brought into the England team aged 20 in 1951, Statham had bowled fewer than 300 first-class overs. But his opening spell for Lancashire in the 1950 Roses match convinced watching selectors that here was a lad to watch. Statham – balanced, double-jointed, and extremely accurate – went on to take 250 Test wickets.

47

Statham was the steady rock in fast-bowling partnerships for England with Frank Tyson and Fred Trueman

Statham *factfile*

Born: 17.6.30, Lancashire
Country: England
Tests: 70 **Wickets:** 252
Average: 24.84

Bobby Simpson

Bobby Simpson's father played soccer for Stenhousemuir in Scotland. His emigration to Australia was the best thing that ever happened to cricket down under. For 40 years, Bobby dominated the game as a batsman, a bowler, a peerless slip fielder, captain and finally a shrewd coach. It took him 52 innings to score the first of his 10 Test hundreds, although it was worth waiting for. After nearly 13 hours against England in 1964, he scored 311. He captained Australia 39 times and lost only 12 matches. Although he retired from international cricket in 1968, Simpson's last match as captain was in 1977-78. With Australian cricket decimated by the Packer circus, Simpson, aged 41, led a young side against India and West Indies. Although beaten by the West Indies, his two centuries against India helped the Australians to a remarkable 3-2 series victory.

Great Scot: Tartan Aussie Bobby Simpson

Simpson *factfile*

Born: 3.2.36, New South Wales
Country: Australia
Tests: 62
Runs: 4869
Hundreds: 10
Average: 46.81

48

49

Harold Larwood

As the bowler who primarily terrorised Australia with his fearsome bowling in the notorious 1932-33 Bodyline series, Harold Larwood was surprisingly diminutive. He stood just 5ft 7ins, but made up for his lack of stature with a fast run-up and shoulders strengthened by two years down the pits in Yorkshire. But in the Bodyline series, in which England captain Douglas Jardine instructed him to bowl bouncers at the leg side, Larwood's principal weapon was devastating accuracy. He took 33 of his 78 Test wickets, including Don Bradman's four times. Sixteen Australian batsmen were clean bowled, the rest peppered around the ribcage into submission. England won the series, Australia threatened to leave the Commonwealth, and Larwood – through a combination of injury and cricket expediency – never played for England again.

Larwood *factfile*

Born: 14.11.04, Nottinghamshire
Died: 22.7.95
Country: England
Tests: 21 **Wickets:** 78
Average: 28.35

PLAYER'S CIGARETTES

D. R. JARDINE (SURREY)

Jardine *factfile*

Born: 23.10.1900, India
Died: 18.6.58
Country: England
Tests: 22 **Runs:** 1296
Hundreds: 1 **Average:** 48.00

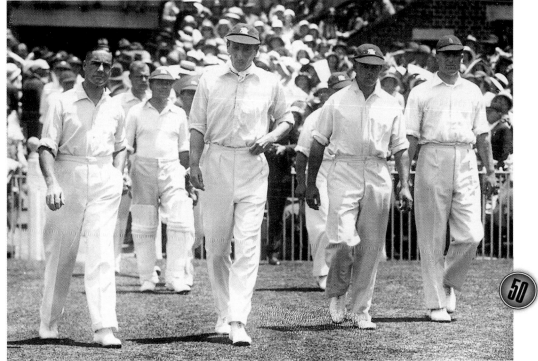

50

Douglas Jardine

Few captains have been so vilified as Douglas Jardine. Then again, few have been so successful. Faced with the prospect of being mauled by Don Bradman in the 1932-33 Ashes series in Australia, Jardine instructed his fast bowlers to aim for a leg-side field that often consisted of six close fielders. For all the repercussions of 'Bodyline', Jardine remained adamant: he had won the series 3-1 and the threat of Bradman had been temporarily extinguished. "As a race, we run ourselves down and write ourselves off at any mention of efficiency and rationalisation," he said later. Indeed, the defeat in Melbourne was the only one under Jardine. The following season he won against the West Indies – scoring a century against some fearsome 'Bodyline' bowling – and he also led his team to India. When the Australians arrived in 1934, it was expected that Jardine would lead the side. But he refused to compromise to the orders of the MCC committee not to repeat the tactics, and resigned the captaincy. He did not play for England or Surrey again.

Douglas Jardine, England's most controversial captain, leads his team out in the Second Test at Melbourne in 1933

Aravinda de Silva

The most exciting batsman Sri Lanka has produced, Aravinda de Silva had, before his 26th birthday, made 267 – the highest Test score by a Sri Lankan in a Test Match – scored the most centuries and was captain of his country. Already a high scorer in English club matches, he made his Test debut against England in 1984. Two years later he made his maiden Test century against Pakistan, having the temerity to reach treble figures with a six off Imran Khan. Back in England in 1991, his 42 on the evening of the Lord's Test was breathtaking, full of invention and delicacy. But the moment of glory for de Silva – who stands just 5ft 3ins – was Sri Lanka's victory over Australia in the World Cup Final in Lahore in 1996. His sparkling innings of 107 against fast bowlers Reiffel and Fleming was truly awesome.

De Silva *factfile*

Born: 17.10.65, Colombo
Country: Sri Lanka
Tests: 70 **Runs:** 4852
Hundreds: 16 **Average:** 42.93

Going for gold: De Silva in textbook form, left, playing against India at Taunton in the 1999 World Cup. Above: On his way to becoming the first Sri Lankan to reach 5000 runs during his 152 against England at The Oval in 1998

Allan Border

Allan Border was a loyal Australian player and captain through the most turbulent times in his country's cricketing history. The fact that he excelled in both, and eventually led Australia out of the wilderness towards their current world standing, is testament to the man.

He made his debut against England in 1978-79 as one of a number of newcomers in an Australian side decimated by defections to Kerry Packer. Australia were thrashed, but Border impressed. His first century came in the following series against Pakistan. When the Packer players, led by Greg Chappell, returned to the fold in 1979-80, Border retained his place and against Pakistan became the first player to score 150 in both innings of a Test match.

In 1981, he was one of very few tourists to shine in England, and when beleaguered Kim Hughes stood down after the West Indies tour, Border was the popular successor. Once again, he had to overcome turmoil as many of his best players fled on the rebel tour to South Africa. But with typical, nuggety determination, he forged a promising new team which won the 1987 World Cup and came to fruition with back-to-back Ashes victories in 1989 and 1990-91.

52

Borderline: The Australian captain slays another English bowler at The Oval

Border *factfile*

Born: 27.7.55, New South Wales
Country: Australia
Tests: 156
Runs: 11174
Hundreds: 27
Average: 50.56

53

Ian Chappell

Oh brother: The oldest of the Chappells, Ian, in action in the Courage Cup at The Oval, in September 1979

A decent batsman and brilliant slip fielder, Ian Chappell's genius was in captaincy. Under him, Australia were transformed from one of the worst to one of the best sides in the world. Of 30 Tests, he won 15, lost five and drew 10. He won series against Pakistan and West Indies, and wrested the Ashes from England, keeping them from both Tony Grieg and Mike Denness. Typically, his reign was not without controversy. Sledging was encouraged, as was a disregard for dress codes and formality. Chappell himself was fined on many occasions for what he did and said to officials. Nevertheless, it was what he did on the pitch that mattered.

Chappell *factfile*

Born: 26.9.43, South Australia
Country: Australia
Tests: 75 **Runs:** 5345
Hundreds: 14 **Average:** 42.42

Bert Sutcliffe

Like his great Yorkshire namesake, Bert Sutcliffe was a batsman of supreme skill. Despite playing with a weak New Zealand team against some of the best teams in the world, Sutcliffe still managed to score five Test centuries and amass 2727 runs. His moment of glory came in the 1955-56 series to India, where he hit two centuries and his 230 not out in Delhi was the highest score made for New Zealand in Test cricket at the time. At the age of 43 he was recalled for the 1965 tours of India, Pakistan and England – and made 151 not out in Calcutta.

Piledriver: The great New Zealand batsman Bert Sutcliffe takes on England at Old Trafford in 1958

Sutcliffe *factfile*

Born: 17.11.23, Auckland
Country: New Zealand
Tests: 42
Runs: 2727
Hundreds: 5
Average: 40.10

54

(55)

Jack Russell

*L*ike all the great wicketkeepers, Jack Russell is nimble behind the stumps, possessed of lightning reflexes, and able to hang around a bit at the crease when the going gets tough. It is the latter aspect of his game which has got England out of trouble on many occasions and why many observers believe that, at the age of 36, he should still be part of the international set-up. Indeed on his debut against Sri Lanka in 1988, it was his batting rather than his wicketkeeping which won the day, Russell scoring 94 as a nightwatchman. The following year, 1989, he scored 64 – the highest score in the doomed England innings – in the Lord's Test against Australia. His most glorious resistance came against South Africa in 1996 when he and Mike Atherton stuck around for five hours to salvage a draw in the Second Test in South Africa. It was the most valuable 29 he has ever scored.

Jack in the box: Russell makes a claim during Gloucestershire's victory over Yorkshire in the 1999 B&H Super Cup at Lord's

Russell *factfile*

Born: 15.8.63, Gloucestershire
Country: England
Tests: 54
Runs: 1897
Hundreds: 2
Average: 27.10
Catches: 153
Stumpings: 12

Jonty Rhodes

Rhodes *factfile*

Born: 27.7.69, Natal
Country: South Africa
Tests: 44
Runs: 2114
Hundreds: 3
Average: 34.65

Above: Jonty Rhodes, acknowledged as the best fielder in the world, takes a spectacular catch against England

There are few fantasy cricket teams these days which do not contain Jonty Rhodes. Quite simply, he is the greatest fielder currently playing, and perhaps of all time. He is perhaps best summed up by a piece of brilliance during the World Cup in 1992 against Pakistan. Chasing eight an over, Inzamam had clubbed a fast 48 off 45 balls. Having driven to square cover, he set off after a quick single but Imran Khan waved him back. Rhodes scooped up the bobbling ball and launched himself horizontally at the stumps from more than 20 yards and with barely one stump to aim at. Inzamam, still yards out of his crease, was astonished when his stumps were shattered.

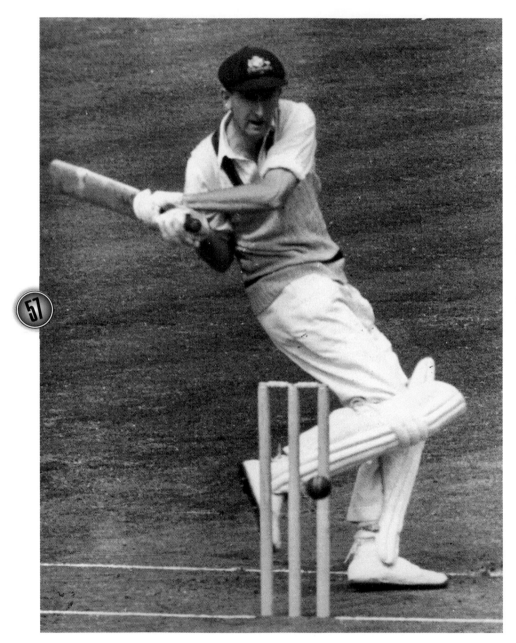

Bill Lawry

Bill Lawry made his debut for Victoria when he was 18, and for Australia in the 1961 Ashes tour when he was 24. He showed sparkling form with the bat, becoming only the third Australian since the War to pass 2,000 runs in an English season. He scored centuries at Lord's and Old Trafford, but these were merely landmarks in a glittering Test career that reaped him 5,234 runs – including 210 against the West Indies.

Unstoppable: Lawry shows his style for Australia against Surrey at The Oval in 1961

Lawry *factfile*

Born: 11.2.37, Victoria
Country: Australia
Tests: 67 **Runs:** 5234
Hundreds: 13
Average: 47.15

Clyde Walcott

58

Along with Frank Worrell and Everton Weekes, Clyde Walcott made up the Three W's who dominated West Indies and world cricket in the 1940s and 1950s. Sturdy and barrel-chested, he possessed a powerful batting style which, between March 1953 and June 1955, helped him to plunder 10 hundreds in 12 Tests against India, England and Australia.

Initially a wicketkeeper – a job which his build never suited – he turned his hand to medium-pace bowling. Although it was never in the same class as his batting, he still managed to claim the scalps of the likes of Len Hutton, Tom Graveney and Neil Harvey. A giant on the pitch, Walcott became an even bigger figure off it. From 1993 until his retirement in 1997, he was Chairman of the International Cricket Council. He was knighted for his services to cricket in Barbados in 1993.

Walcott *factfile*

Born: 17.1.26, Barbados
Country: West Indies
Tests: 44 **Runs:** 3798
Hundreds: 15 **Average:** 56.68

Everton Weekes

L ike a bull terrier, Everton Weekes would snap at the heels of bowlers. And more often than not, he would send them running away down the garden path. Only George Headley has a better average among West Indian batsmen. In innings in 1948 and 1949, against England and India, Weekes scored a record five successive hundreds – and had he not been run out on 90 in Madras, he would have made it six. His batting partner was invariably Frank Worrell. On form, they could end a Test match before it started. Together they punished England at Trent Bridge in 1950 by scoring 283 in just 210 minutes. In 1995, Weekes was given a knighthood for services to cricket.

59

Flying start: In 1950 Weekes and Worrell scored 283 against England in 210 minutes

Weekes *factfile*

Born: 26.2.25, Barbados
Country: West Indies
Tests: 48
Runs: 4455
Hundreds: 15
Average: 58.61

In a cricket-playing country which habitually breeds some of the most frightening fast bowlers in the world, laid-back spinners like Lance Gibbs were something of a rarity. Still, it didn't make him any less deadly. With his incredibly long spinning fingers, he took 309 Test wickets – a feat only surpassed by Shane Warne among slow bowlers. At Old Trafford in 1963, Gibbs produced his best ever Test return of 11 for 157 as the West Indies cruised to victory over England in the First Test. Recognised as one of the best off-spinners the game has known, Gibbs twice took 10 wickets in a match and five in an innings 18 times. His best performance was in India in 1961-2 when he took 8-38 from 53.3 overs. His last Test was in 1976 when, with greying hair, he surpassed Fred Trueman's Test record of 307 wickets.

60

....

The spin king: Lance Gibbs overtook Fred Trueman's Test wicket record haul in his final match

Gibbs *factfile*

Born: 29.9.34, Guyana
Country: West Indies
Tests: 79 **Wickets:** 309
Average: 29.09

Lance Gibbs

Archie Maclaren

There were some towering figures in English cricket at the turn of the century, and none more so than A.C. 'Archie' Maclaren. A batsman of the highest order, Maclaren's style mirrored his autocratic outlook on life and on the game: erect stance, bat held high, strokes dismissed with a flourish as if swatting a fly. He made his first tour to Australia with W.G. Grace's winning side in 1893 when he was 22, and the following year, playing for Lancashire, he scored 424 against Somerset – a record which lasted for 73 years. He led England 22 times, although his three series against the Australians ended in defeat. Like his mentor Grace, Maclaren played on until he was well into his fifties when he led an all-amateur side which famously beat the 1921 Australians.

61

Aristocrat at the crease: Archie Maclaren scored five centuries for England with a style like 'swatting flies'

Maclaren *factfile*

Born: 1.12.1871, Lancashire
Died: 17.11.1944
Country: England
Tests: 35 **Runs:** 1931
Hundreds: 5 **Average:** 33.87

Derek Underwood

Deadly Derek: The remarkable Mr Underwood hails another victim in his mammoth haul of 297 Test wickets

Left arm spinner Derek Underwood was marked out as something special when, aged just 18, he took an unprecedented 100 first-class wickets for Kent. Had he not signed up first with Kerry Packer and them with the rebel South Africa tour he would have undoubtedly become England's leading Test wicket taker. In the event, he took 297 – none more dramatic than the seven he took for just 50 runs in 1968 at the Oval which enabled England to steal a dramatic victory over the Australians. Needing 352 to win, Australia were almost saved by the rain. But when the rain stopped, the crowd helped with the mopping up and Underwood mopped up the rest of the Australian innings.

Underwood *factfile*

Born: 8.6.45, Kent
Country: England
Tests: 86 **Wickets:** 297
Average: 25.83

Clarrie Grimmett

Next time Shane Warne claims a wicket with the 'flipper' delivery, he ought to say a silent prayer of thanks to Clarrie Grimmett, who in the 1920s was the father of Australian spin and who invented the delivery. Grimmett was 33 before he was first capped – but his 11-82 against England in Sydney in 1924-25 made the selectors realise what they had been missing. With his jerky action, accuracy and deceptive flight, Grimmett would go on to become the first bowler ever to take 200 Test wickets. His bowling partnership with Bill O'Reilly was devastating: in 15 Tests together, Grimmett took 88 wickets and O'Reilly 81. Even in his 50s, Grimmett was still perfecting his art.

Grimmett *factfile*

Born: 25.12.1891, Victoria
Died: 2.5.80
Country: Australia **Tests:** 37
Wickets: 216 **Average:** 24.21

Clarrie Grimmett, pictured at the crease against England in 1934

Constantine took nine wickets in the match with his unpredictable bowling. A year earlier, in 1928, he was only one of three touring cricketers this century to do the double of 1,000 runs and 100 wickets in an English season for Nelson in the Lancashire league. In his last match, at The Oval in 1939, he claimed 5-79 followed by 79 in less than an hour as West Indies won.

Lord of the crease: **Sir Learie Constantine** batting against Middlesex during his final tour of England, in 1939

64

Learie Constantine

There were better bowlers and batsmen than Learie Constantine, but no bigger cricketing celebrity. Constantine revelled in the possibilities of the game on and off the field. He loved England,

and England loved him, first as a player, then as an ambassador and lawyer, as a knight and finally as a Lord. It was on the field that he first made an impression. In the West Indies' first Test victory over England, in 1929-30,

Constantine *factfile*

Born: 21.12.02, Barbados
Country: West Indies
Tests: 18 **Runs:** 635
Average: 19.24 **Wickets:** 58
Average: 30.10

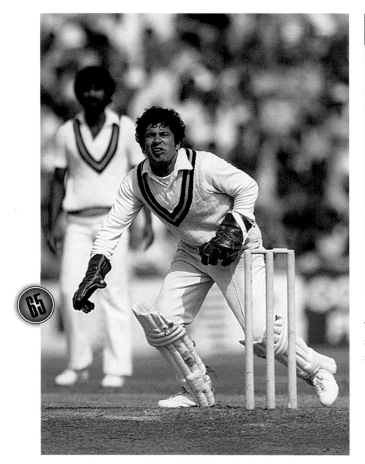

Bari *factfile*

Born: 23.3.48, Karachi
Country: Pakistan
Tests: 81
Runs: 1366
Average: 15.88
Catches: 201
Stumpings: 27

The Bari facts: Wasim took 228 victims behind the stumps for Pakistan

Bob Willis

Eyes bulging, bowling arm flapping behind him like a jockey's whip, Bob Willis provided the lasting image of England's sensational victory over Australia in 1981 at Headingley. If it is Ian Botham who continues to get all the plaudits as the architect of that 18-run victory against all the odds, it was Willis who provided the killer blow with a devastating spell of 8-43.

Willis was a surprising choice as England captain in 1982, and it was a role the Warwickshire paceman never seemed at all comfortable with. He was forced to relinquish leadership to his deputy David Gower on several occasions because of injury, and, after winning seven of the 18 matches under his control, he eventually ceded the captaincy to Gower full time.

It is his all-out pace and determination – and of course that memorable day in 1981 – for which he will be remembered.

All guns blazing: Willis in energetic action on England's tour of India in 1982

Wasim Bari

One of the world's great wicketkeepers, Wasim Bari was the first Asian cricketer to claim 200 dismissals. Against New Zealand in 1979 he took seven catches, a record he still shares with England's Bob Taylor. Wasim led Pakistan in two losing series against England following the defection of many of Pakistan's first-string players to Kerry Packer.

Willis *factfile*

Born: 30.5.49, Tyne and Wear
Country: England
Tests: 90
Wickets: 325
Average: 25.20

Keith Miller

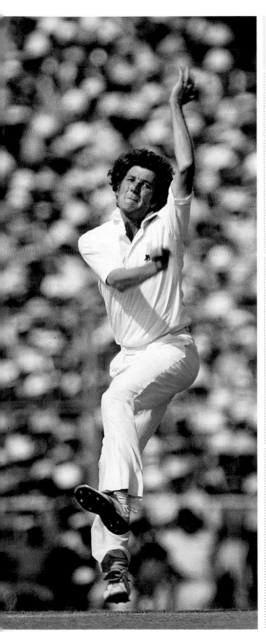

Whether bowling in tandem with Ray Lindwall or smashing sixes on his own, Keith Miller was a dashing cricketer straight out of a *Boy's Own* comic. Indeed, when he appeared in the Victory Tests of 1945 he had only recently returned from the war as a fighter pilot. True to his heroic image, he proceeded to smash 185 in 167 scoring seven sixes, one of which nearly went over the pavilion at Lord's. He was no less deadly with the ball, taking 170 wickets at 22.97. An all-round giant.

Miller *factfile*

Born: 28.11.19, New South Wales
Country: Australia
Tests: 55 **Runs:** 2958
Hundreds: 7 **Average:** 36.97
Wickets: 170 **Average:** 22.97

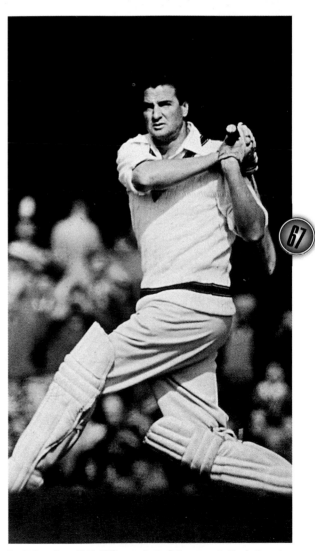

67

Boy's Own hero: Keith Miller was Australia's answer to Denis Compton

Imperious: Dexter in 1960 against South Africa

Alec Bedser

A lec Bedser was a tireless bowler who wore the three lions with pride and would run through brick walls for his team and his country. After his retirement, Bedser the administrator proved as dedicated a servant to English cricket as he was as a player. He was no mean bowler: in successive series against Australia in 1950-51 and 1953 he took 69 wickets at 16.87. Although he was a medium pacer, Bedser had the uncanny

knack of spinning the ball at full whack. Even the great Don Bradman was moved to praise the leg-cutter which removed his off stump in Adelaide in 1946 as "as good a ball as I have ever received".

Bedser *factfile*

Born: 4.7.18, Surrey
Country: England
Tests: 51
Wickets: 236
Average: 24.89

Dexter *factfile*

Born: 15.5.35, Italy
Country: England
Tests: 62 **Runs:** 4502
Hundreds: 9 **Average:** 47.89

Ted Dexter

69

Ted Dexter was born in Milan, and whatever he did – whether on the field or travelling round the grounds on his motorbike as chairman of selectors – he did with typically cool Italian style. At the crease, Dexter was imperious and powerful. He thrived on the very best that the best bowlers could throw at him. At Lord's in 1963 against the West Indies, he faced the might of Wes Hall and Charlie Griffith with glee, smashing them for 70 off 73 balls. As England captain, however, he somehow lacked the spark that typified his batting. When dealing with his own players, he was unable to rid himself of the very aloofness that let him treat bowlers with disdain. Still, when he retired aged just 30, it was a great loss to the England team.

Colin Cowdrey

70

Cowdrey took over the captaincy from Mike Smith but then lost it to Brian Close. After Close had a run-in with a spectator the following year, Cowdrey was finally given the command he craved, and celebrated in the West Indies by scoring two centuries. Things got even better the following summer when he led an Ashes-winning side. But, after being named captain for a tour to New Zealand, Cowdrey tore his achilles tendon in a Sunday league match and was replaced by Ray Illingworth. He never regained the captaincy – but such was his dedication to the cause he made his last Test performance aged 42 when called out as emergency cover to the West Indies in 1974-75. He would later become President of the MCC and was knighted in 1991.

England stalwart: The great Colin Cowdrey

A brilliant yet introspective batsman, Colin Cowdrey always aspired to but was consistently denied the England captaincy. When he did finally get it, his reign was all too brief. After making his debut under Len Hutton in Australia in 1954-55, Cowdrey spent many years as Peter May's deputy. But when May relinquished command, captaincy went to Ted Dexter. In 1966,

Cowdrey *factfile*

Born: 24.12.32, India
Country: England
Tests: 114
Runs: 7624
Hundreds: 22
Average: 44.06

Neil Harvey

Neil Harvey announced himself as a batsman of genius at Headingley in 1948 when he became the first left-hander to score 100 in his first Test against England. By the time he was 21 he had scored five hundreds and had a Test average of 120. Such was his prowess and reliability, he remained first choice for his country for the next 15 years – and captained it once in the absence of Richie Benaud. Although he loved to race the runs, his finest innings was the ground-out undefeated 151 on a turning pitch in Durban in 1949-50 with which he helped Australia beat South Africa.

71

Harvey *factfile*

Born: 8.10.28, Victoria
Country: Australia
Tests: 79 **Runs:** 6149
Hundreds: 21 **Average:** 48.41

Dressed for success: Neil Harvey averaged nearly 50 in Tests

Jeff Thomson

For batsmen playing Australia, it just didn't seem fair. First there was Dennis Lillee, now there was Jeff Thomson as well. In the 1970s, 'Lillian Thomson' destroyed batting attacks – and never more so than England's in 1974-75, when Thommo took 33 wickets in five Tests. He bowled with a devastating slingshot action that, in many batmen's opinion, propelled the ball faster than anyone else in history. Sadly, injury limited him to just 200 Test wickets.

72

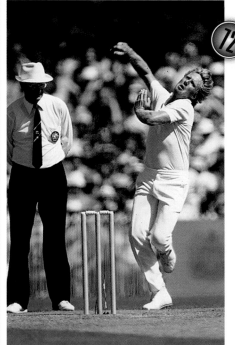

Ready or not, here I come: Thommo in action

Waqar Younis

Batsmen will not thank Waqar Younis for his gift to the game. Reverse swing, where the ball swings against the shine, bowled at high speed and full length, caused absolute mayhem when the Pakistan paceman introduced it to an unsuspecting world in 1990. Indeed, with it, he recorded a remarkable 190 wickets in his first 33 Tests. And just when batsmen thought they were getting the hang of it, Waqar had another trick up his sleeve: the in-swinging yorker. In tandem with Wasim Akram, Waqar was one of the most devastating bowlers of all time until injury began to take its toll.

73

Younis *factfile*

Born: 16.11.71, Vehari
Country: Pakistan
Tests: 53
Wickets: 267
Average: 21.52

The destroyer: Waqar at work in Sharjah in October 1991, before injury – and the arrival of Shoaib Akhtar – forced him out of the spotlight

Thomson *factfile*

Born: 16.8.50, New South Wales
Country: Australia
Tests: 51
Wickets: 200
Average: 28.01

Allan Donald

Allan Donald was a fast bowler of the old school, and his duel with Mike Atherton at Trent Bridge in the vital Fourth Test in 1998 was a throwback to classic head-to-heads of yesteryear. Donald, the sharpshooting South African bowler, was on his last tour of England and desperate to end it with a win. In the end it was Atherton who came out top dog – although one felt that Donald deserved his last moment of glory after helping South Africa to the forefront of world cricket for the first time since their return from the wilderness. Worthy of comparison with all the greats, his strike rate of a wicket every 47 balls is exceptional.

White lightning: Allan Donald in World Cup 99

Donald *factfile*

Born: 20.10.66, Bloemfontein
Country: South Africa
Tests: 42 **Wickets:** 204 **Average:** 22.45

Malcolm Marshall

Bristling with aggression, Malcolm Marshall was a pocket dynamo. Although he was physically opposite to the likes of Garner, Holding and Roberts, he still finished with well over 100 more wickets than them and at a far cheaper rate. He took 1,637 first-class wickets – the only comparable bowlers are Fred Trueman and Brian Statham.

74

75

Wes Hall

Wes Hall took over 190 Test wickets – but his importance to West Indies cricket was that his thunderous, flailing style was a precursor to the era of Holding, Garner and Ambrose. His run-up was so long that he was very nearly at the boundary, and his follow-through took him almost up to the batsman. He was a workhorse: in India and Pakistan in 1958-59 he took 46 wickets in eight Tests at just under 18 apiece. Later, he would become Minister for Sport and Tourism in Barbados, as well as a well-liked team manager of the West Indies.

Hall *factfile*

Born: 12.9.37, Barbados
Country: West Indies
Tests: 48 **Wickets:** 192
Average: 26.38

Small but deadly: Malcolm Marshall was a vital component of West Indies' four-man pace attack

Marshall *factfile*

Born: 18.4.58, Barbados
Country: West Indies
Tests: 81
Wickets: 376
Average: 20.94

76

John Reid

Peter May

The great New Zealand captain John Reid put so much effort into raising the profile of his side in the world game, it is amazing he found time to perform the miracles he did. Reid led his side on 34 consecutive occasions from 1955, a record beaten only by Border and Sobers. He batted, bowled, fielded and kept wicket, and very probably brought the drinks on at the interval. In 1955-56, he led New Zealand to their first ever Test win, against the West Indies. And in 1961-62 in South Africa, Reid cut loose, scoring 1,915 runs at 68.39 to lead his side to a first overseas victory.

77

Leading from the front: John Reid saves New Zealand from defeat at The Oval in 1949. He would later captain New Zealand 34 times

Reid *factfile*

Born: 3.6.28, Auckland
Country: New Zealand
Tests: 58 **Runs:** 3428
Hundreds: 6 **Average:** 33.28

78

Tall and elegant, with a range of classical strokes at his disposal, Peter May was the archetypal English batsman – and one of the best of the post-war era. He led England to 20 Test victories with quiet determination. He was often perceived as arrogant and aloof by the Press, but among his peers he was highly respected. It was a great loss when his career was cut short by illness when he was just 32.

May's Test debut was marked by a brilliant 138 against South Africa in 1951, and the highlight was 285 not out against India in 1958. His on-drive made him the scourge of

Gordon Greenidge

At his best, and usually in cahoots with opening partner Desmond Haynes, Gordon Greenidge was one of the most exciting and dynamic opening batsmen in Test cricket. Born in Barbados, he played for England schools – but then elected to play Test cricket for West Indies. It was a terrible loss. On his Test debut against India in 1973-74 he made 93 and 107 runs while another debutant, Viv Richards, made just seven. Over the next few years, Greenidge's performances would taunt England about the one that got away. On the 1976 tour to England, he scored 592 at 65, including a century in each innings on a poor Old Trafford pitch. In 1984, on the same ground, he blasted a double hundred against England as the West Indies crushed the home side. In all, he scored 19 Test hundreds. When not playing for the West Indies he was partnering Barry Richards at Hampshire – one of the most daunting double acts in any team.

Peter May and Colin Cowdrey leave the field during their world record partnership of 411 to save the 1957 Edgbaston Test against Sonny Ramadhin and the West Indies. May went on to score 285 not out

bowlers throughout the world. He would later hold every high office in the game, but in his latter years he often found himself at odds with modern players who regarded him as old-fashioned and out of touch.

May *factfile*

Born: 31.12.29, Berkshire
Died: 27.12.94
Country: England
Tests: 66
Runs: 4537
Hundreds: 13
Average: 46.77

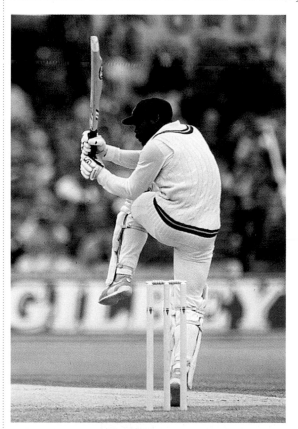

Maverick: Greenidge blasting past 200 at Old Trafford in 1984

79

Greenidge *factfile*

Born: 1.5.51, Barbados
Country: West Indies
Tests: 108 **Runs:** 7558
Hundreds: 19 **Average:** 44.72

Geoff Howarth

Until the 1999 touring party won in England, New Zealand's most successful era was under Geoff Howarth's captaincy in the 1970s. Among mediocre batsman, he shone like a beacon, scoring a century in each innings against England at Auckland in 1977-78, 123 against England at Lords in 1978 and a century against Pakistan later that year. His bravado with the bat led to him being appointed captain against the West Indies in 1979-80. Under Howarth, New Zealand did not lose a home series, beating the West Indies and India and winning at Headingley in 1983 – their first win in England and the first abroad since 1969. Later that year, under Howarth's inspired leadership, New Zealand got their revenge, beating England in a rubber for the first time in 21 attempts.

80

Inspirational: Geoff Howarth lifted New Zealand to unknown heights

Howarth *factfile*

Born: 29.3.51, Auckland
Country: New Zealand
Tests: 47 **Runs:** 2531
Hundreds: 6 **Average:** 32.44

Derek Randall

With his familiar exhortation of "Coom on, Rags!", Derek Randall was one of England's best-loved players. The Nottinghamshire man had a style of his own, whether batting face on with his legs astride, or cavorting in the field.

He played 47 Tests, but for some reason never instilled total confidence in the selectors. But if Randall occasionally came across as the village idiot, there were few in the game who could match his athleticism, his eye for a run-out or his guts with the bat. His 174 in the Centenary Test in 1977 against Australia at Melbourne showed precisely what he was made of.

81

Madcap genius: Derek Randall, the great entertainer

Rohan Kanhai

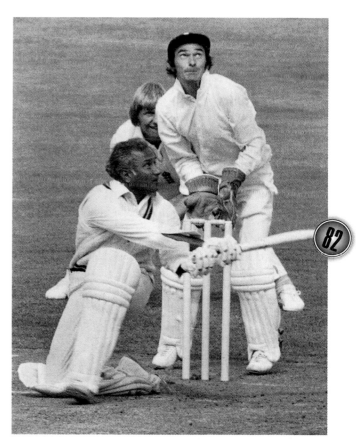

With 15 Test hundreds to his name, there was no doubting Rohan Kanhai was a brilliant batsman. But it was his style which made him such an appealing player to watch. He believed that if a ball was there to be hit, it should be hit hard. He possessed tremendous power; some of his hook shots reached the boundary in the blink of an eye. His maiden Test hundred was a thunderous 256 at Calcutta in 1958-59, and in the next Test he was run out for 99. As a captain, he was often as pugnacious as his shot-making. At Edgbaston in 1973, the umpire refused to take to the field at the start of

The godfather: Rohan Kanhai sweeps Underwood at Lord's in 1973, during his century on the first day

the third day after getting a mouthful from Kanhai for not giving Geoff Boycott out. Kanhai later apologised, and went on to thrash 157 at Lord's to secure a 2-0 series win.

Randall *factfile*

Born: 24.2.51, Nottinghamshire
Country: England
Tests: 47 **Runs:** 2470
Hundreds: 7 **Average:** 33.37

Kanhai *factfile*

Born: 26.12.35, British Guyana
Country: West Indies
Tests: 79 **Runs:** 6227 **Hundreds:** 15
Average: 47.53

Javed Miandad

iery and pugnacious, Javed Miandad translated his natural inclinations into batting and his captaincy of Pakistan. He was never far from controversy, almost coming to blows with Dennis Lillee during a tour to Australia in 1982 and sacked by his county Glamorgan for failing to return on time after hitting the winning runs in a one-day international in Sharjah. Yet Miandad could always answer his critics with his performances on the field. At the age of 19 he scored 163 on his Pakistan debut against New Zealand in 1976, and became the youngest ever batsman to score a double century when he made 206 later in the series. At 22, he was Pakistan's youngest captain (against Australia), but such was his temperament, he was forced to relinquish the position by the rest of his team for the next series.

In the next 10 years he would captain his side 28 times, winning 11 matches and upsetting both Mike Gatting and Allan Border with his gamesmanship. Yet it was this streetwise attitude, allied to superlative batting skills, which helped Pakistan rise to their current position in world cricket.

Street fighter: The volcanic Javed Miandad in Sharjah in 1991

Miandad *factfile*

Born: 12.6.57, Karachi
Country: Pakistan
Tests: 109 **Runs:** 8064
Hundreds: 22 **Average:** 54.85

John Snow

ast bowler John Snow cemented his reputation with sensational performances between 1968 and 1971 against the West Indies and Australia. Having been omitted from the first Test in the Caribbean in 1967-68 because of inconsistency, Snow returned in the second and third Tests with a point to prove, skittling seven

83

84

Bill Ponsford

Snow storm: The England quickie found fame in the West Indies, where he outgunned Hall and Griffith

and eight wickets respectively to help England win the series. In Australia in 1970-71, he took 31 wickets including 7-40 in the fourth Test in Sydney as England, under Ray Illingworth, won the series.

If Bill Ponsford was ever peeved that it was Bradman, not he, who received all the adoration for making huge scores, then he had a point. Ponsford is still the only batsman to have made two scores of over 400, in State matches in Australia. Indeed, it was in Sheffield Shield matches that he tended to rake in the runs: in 1927 he scored 1,146 runs from five games for Victoria at an extraordinary average of 229.20.

The year before, he scored 352 against New South Wales. When he and Bradman did come together, it was inevitable that they would make runs, and they did – 388 and 451

Run king: Les Ames watches Ponsford at The Oval in 1934, where he made 266 and Bradman 244

at Headingley and The Oval in 1934. Ironically, in that series, Ponsford averaged 94.83 to Bradman's 94.73.

85

The great C B Fry once remarked of the Indian batsman K.S. Ranjitsinhji that "he has three strokes for every ball". That is how it must have seemed to the opposition as the slim-built 'Ranji' revolutionised batting and delighted crowds, becoming the first non-white sportsman to achieve international celebrity.

Born in India but educated in England, Ranji's style was so unorthodox it took him four years to get a game in the first XI at Cambridge University. Some observers claimed he was little more than a conjuror.

86

Adopted by Sussex, he twice made 3000 runs in a season. In his first Test match for England against Australia in 1896 (India would not play Test cricket

Ranjitsinhji

until 1932) he made 62 and 154 not out, and 175 in his first Test match in Australia in 1897-98. Although he made little money out of cricket, the game transformed his life when, in 1907, he was elected to the throne of Nawanagar in his homeland.

Ranjitsinhji *factfile*

Born: 10.9.1872, Sarodar
Died: 2.4.1933
Country: India
Tests: 15
Runs: 989
Hundreds: 2
Average: 44.95

Tony Greig

South African-born Tony Greig towered at 6ft 7ins, and for 58 Tests – 14 as captain – he towered over the English game. A great all-rounder, he scored eight Test centuries and brought a vibrancy and bullishness to England that had been missing for some time. Installed as captain in 1975, he provoked the same mixed feelings as Douglas Jardine: he was successful, but his means often annoyed his masters. Yet he instilled backbone into the England side. His first

Greig *factfile*

Born: 6.10.46, South Africa
Country: England
Tests: 58 **Runs:** 3599
Hundreds: 8 **Average:** 40.43
Wickets: 141 **Average:** 32.20

Bhagwat Chandrasekhar

87

88

Nets in Melbourne for 1979 Super Test

series was drawn in Australia, the next was a resounding win in India. Before the 1976 series against West Indies, he ill-advisedly said he would make the tourists 'grovel'. They didn't and this turned many against him.

When it became clear he was negotiating with Kerry Packer, his standing fell further and he was regarded as a traitor to English cricket – even though he was merely trying to get a better deal for poorly-paid cricketers. He lost the captaincy to Mike Brearley in 1977 and became Packer's leading light.

B hagwat Chandrasekhar was stricken with polio when he was five, yet turned his affliction into an advantage to become one of the great leg-break bowlers of all time. Holding the ball in both hands as he ran up, rather like a bowls player, he would unleash a selection of spinners all at virtually slow-medium pace. Like an Indian fakir, he mesmerised batsmen before getting them out. He registered 242 wickets at 29.74 in 58 Tests. His figures of 12 for 104 in

Melbourne in 1978 secured India's first win on Australian soil. Against England at The Oval in 1971, his second innings stint of 6-38 gave India victory by four wickets.

Chandrasekhar *factfile*

Born: 17.5.45, Bangalore
Country: India
Tests: 58 **Wickets:** 242 **Average:** 29.74

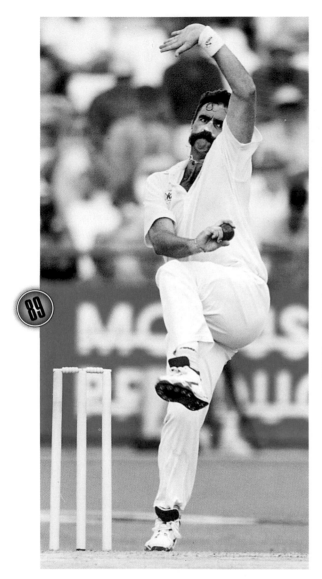

Although pilloried and hero-worshipped in equal measure for his bushy moustache and lager-swilling Aussie outback mentality, Merv Hughes was a class act who made a fool out of anyone who didn't take him seriously. Stung by a disastrous debut against India, in which he returned figures of 1-123 and was out for a duck, Hughes fought back with a brilliant 13-wicket haul against the West Indies in 1987. And on his second tour to England in 1993, he became only the seventh Australian bowler to take 200 wickets.

Bristling with hostility: Merv Hughes

Hughes *factfile*

Born: 23.11.61, Victoria
Country: Australia
Tests: 53
Wickets: 212 **Average:** 28.38

89

Merv Hughes

Ray Illingworth

An accomplished middle-order batsman and occasionally deadly off-break bowler, Raymond Illingworth's forte was brilliant tactical captaincy. In 31 Tests, he lost only five and, significantly, not only won the Ashes in 1970-71 but successfully defended them in 1972. "Illingworth was the best captain I've ever played under," said Alan Knott, who played under Mike Brearley, Colin Cowdrey and Tony Greig. "He knew everything about the game and the techniques of his opponents and he thrived on pressure, as bowler, batsman and captain."

90

Ken Barrington

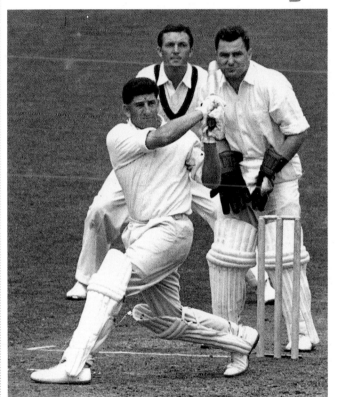

father figure to the players and the world of cricket was stunned when he died suddenly of a heart attack during a Test match in Barbados in 1981.

Heart of oak: The doughty Englishman Barrington strikes out for Surrey against Australia, watched by Benaud in the slips and wicketkeeper Jarman

91

Headingley hero: Illingworth is congratulated by Gary Sobers, opposite, on England's 2-0 series win in 1969

Illingworth factfile

Born: 8.6.42, Yorkshire
Country: England
Tests: 61
Wickets: 122
Average: 31.20

Craggy-faced and lion-hearted, Ken Barrington scored 20 Test hundreds and bowled well enough to count Gary Sobers and Clyde Walcott among his victims. But it was on the special buzz of an Ashes series that Barrington thrived. In 39 innings against Australia, he averaged 63.96 – more than Len Hutton and Geoffrey Boycott. As England coach, he became a

Barrington factfile

Born: 24.11.30, Surrey
Died: 14.3.81
Country: England
Tests: 82 **Runs:** 6806
Hundreds: 20
Average: 58.67

Maurice Tate

Bishen Bedi

O ne of the best slow left-arm bowlers, whose action never failed to have the connoisseurs drooling, Bishen Bedi was also one of India's most outspoken captains. With his trademark turban, he made his debut in 1966 against the West Indies,

Turban guerrilla: A rare shot of Bedi without his titfer

Tate *factfile*

Born: 30.5.1895, Sussex
Died: 18.5.56
Country: England
Tests: 39
Wickets: 155
Average: 26.16

M aurice Tate was the first bowler to make full use of the seam, and such was the way he swung the ball, he had to wear a reinforced corset to protect his body as it twisted round. Still, he was mightily effective, taking 155 wickets in 39 Tests at an average of 26.16. He enjoyed particular success in Australia in 1924-25, where he took 38 wickets at 23.18 – a record for a visiting player. Big, powerful and tireless, he bowled twice as many overs that series as anyone else and on his return was dubbed the greatest bowler in the world.

Bedi *factfile*

Born: 25.9.46, Amritsar
Country: India
Tests: 67
Wickets: 266
Average: 28.71

Martin Crowe

Spin doctor: Bedi the conjuror in action in 1971

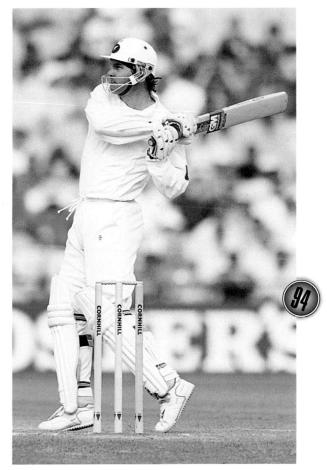

*I*n tandem with Richard Hadlee, Martin Crowe made New Zealand a team to be respected in the 1980s. Crowe is without doubt the finest batsman his country has produced. He made his first Test century against England in 1984 and has since scored more Test hundreds than any New Zealand batsman. In his first Test as captain, against Sri Lanka, he hit 299 – a New Zealand record. A bold captain, whose tactics included opening his one-day attack with spin, he took New Zealand to the 1992 World Cup semi-finals.

Kiwi takes wing: Crowe facing England at Old Trafford in 1994

scoring 67. Controversy was never far behind, however. In 1974, while on tour to England, he led a faction protesting for more money.

On his return to India, he was banned for one match for giving a live TV interview. Backed by other players, he was appointed captain after India's disastrous performances in the 1975 World Cup. In 1976, during a match against the West Indies in Jamaica, Bedi declared the Indian innings closed in protest against intimidatory bowling which put five of his players out of the game.

He later managed India, and was never far from the hotbed of political intrigue behind the scenes of Indian cricket.

Crowe *factfile*

Born: 22.9.62, Auckland
Country: New Zealand
Tests: 56
Runs: 3993
Hundreds: 13
Average: 48.10

Hanif Mohammed

95

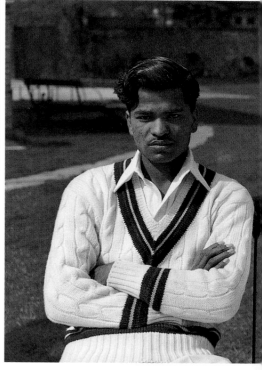

Small and frail-looking, Hanif Mohammed was nevertheless a batsman of great vigilance and determination who would stay in all day if necessary. His two greatest batting feats bear witness to his tenacity. In 1960, playing for Karachi against Bahawalpur, he scored 499 – the highest ever score until Brian Lara's monster knock 35 years later. In 1958, he scored 337 for Pakistan against the West Indies in 16 hours and 10 minutes – a record which survives today by three hours. The score secured an unlikely draw for Pakistan, who had followed on 473 runs behind. But that was Hanif's style. He thrived on lost causes, such as the 187 not out against England at Lord's in 1967 which, again, helped secure a draw after Pakistan were 99 for six. Hanif's son Shoaib was also a Test player.

Hanif *factfile*

Born: 21.12.34, Karachi
Country: Pakistan
Tests: 55 **Runs:** 3915
Hundreds: 12 **Average:** 43.98

The limpet: Once Hanif got his eye in, he was impossible to get out

Wire-thin, with his cap pulled down on his head and his sleeves rolled down, Sonny Ramadhin looked for all the world like a schoolboy bowler. Yet in 1950 at Lord's, he taught England's much-vaunted batsmen a lesson.

Unable to work out whether he was bowling leg-breaks or off-breaks, England were routed and Ramadhin ended up with the extraordinary figures of 115-70-152-11. Alf Valentine mopped up the remaining nine wickets and the West Indies had won their first ever Test in England.

Spin twins: Ramadhin, right, with Alf Valentine, 1950

Brian Close

From the same bullish Yorkshire mould as Geoffrey Boycott, Brian Close had a knack of getting up the noses of officialdom. Yet when the going got tough, officialdom would always call upon Close to save the day. He rarely let them down. A hard-hitting left-hand batsman, right-arm bowler and one of the most courageous close-in fielders in the game, Close captained England to victory over India and Pakistan in 1967 and was set to lead the side to the Caribbean the following winter. But, after using delaying tactics to prevent Warwickshire winning a vital county championship match, Close had a bust-up with a spectator. He was carpeted by the MCC and dropped from the side.

True to form, he returned to help England against the rampant West Indies in 1976. Aged 45, he was battered from pillar to post, but unlike the rest of the team, refused to bend.

Courage: Facing West Indies in 1976

Sonny Ramadhin

Ramadhin *factfile*

Born: 1.5.29, Trinidad
Country: West Indies
Tests: 43 **Wickets:** 158 **Average:** 28.98

Close *factfile*

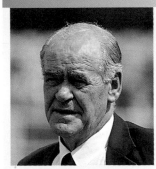

Born: 24.2.31, Yorkshire
Country: England
Tests: 22 **Runs:** 887
Hundreds: 0 **Average:** 25.34

Mike Brearley

Intelligent, articulate and an unrivalled man-manager, Mike Brearley took the art of captaincy to previously unknown heights during his tenure from 1977-81. Stepping into the breach after Tony Greig's links with Kerry Packer were revealed, he led England to victory over Australia in 1977, and over Pakistan and New Zealand in 1978. In Australia in 1978-79 England won the Ashes 5-1.

Brearley retired in 1980, but was hastily recalled after England, under Ian Botham, slumped against the Aussies in 1981.

Brearley's triumph was to motivate the dejected

Botham and persuade him and the rest of the team that they were the world-beaters they would subsequently prove to be in the rest of that series, which England won 3-1.

The professor: Brearley – now a working psychologist – used his academic skills to motivate England, bringing the best out of Ian Botham and Bob Willis

98

Brearley *factfile*

Born: 28.4.42, Middlesex
Country: England
Tests: 39
Runs: 1442
Hundreds: 0
Average: 22.88

Mike Gatting

Bearded and belligerent, in his prime Mike Gatting was capable of smashing holes in most attacks. He made his Test debut in Pakistan in 1977-78, but despite many near-misses it was not until 54 Tests later, in Bombay in 1984-85, that he made his first century. A double century followed later in that series and from there he would go on to make nine hundreds.

His captaincy was a rather more chequered affair. After losing series against India and New Zealand, he led England to a surprise Ashes win over Allan Border's Australia in 1986-87.

In 1987-88 it all went pear-shaped. First, there was the row with Pakistani umpire Shakoor Rana. Then lurid headlines about his private life lost him the captaincy during the West Indies series.

He was eventually banned after leading a rebel tour to South Africa but returned to Test cricket just in time to be spectacularly bowled by Shane Warne in 1993.

99

Pugnacious: Gatting was the typical British bulldog

Gatting *factfile*

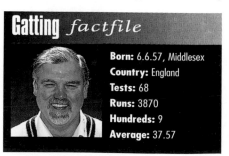

Born: 6.6.57, Middlesex
Country: England
Tests: 68
Runs: 3870
Hundreds: 9
Average: 37.57

Alvin Kallicharran

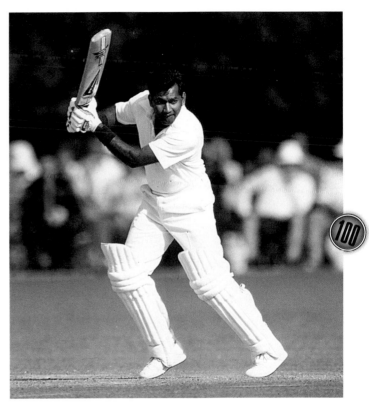

100

There were few players of such delicacy and fluency as Alvin Kallicharran. Yet he needed all his fancy footwork to lead the West Indies through the biggest crisis in their history.

Having scored a century on his Test debut against New Zealand in 1971-72 he followed this with another in the second Test. Altogether he would make 12 Test tons of the highest order, but he found trouble ahead in 1977 when, with the rest of Clive Lloyd's side, he signed for Kerry Packer.

He was forced to withdraw due to a sponsorship wrangle, however, and found himself captain of the second-string players that remained. Despite this, he continued to show masterly form with the bat in Australia and India, scoring in all over 4,400 Test runs. It was only when Lloyd returned in 1979 that his form declined.

Century star: Kallicharran made 12 tons in 66 Tests

Kallicharran *factfile*

Born: 21.3.49, British Guyana
Country: West Indies
Tests: 66
Runs: 4399
Hundreds: 12
Average: 44.43

In 1997, in his book *From Arlott to Aggers: 40 Years of Test Match Special*, Peter Baxter asked all the BBC Radio cricket commentators to choose their Dream Teams since 1957, when the programme started.

Jonathan Agnew, Trevor Bailey, Peter Baxter, Henry Blofeld, Chris Cowdrey, Tony Cozier, Gerald de Kock, Graeme Fowler, Bill Frindall, Robert Hudson, David Lloyd, Vic Marks, Christopher Martin-Jenkins, Don Mosey, Neville Oliver, Mike Selvey, E.W. Swanton and Bryan Waddle all submitted their ideal teams.

From these individual teams, an ultimate TMS Dream Team was compiled, based on the number of votes cast. We are pleased to reproduce it here.

● The Test Match Special 40th Anniversary Dream Team ●

Selected by the TMS commentary team

'The most complete opening batsman I have seen. Brave against fast bowling and quick, nimble and assertive against the spinners, which is by no means usual for an opener.'
Jonathan Agnew
on Sunil Gavaskar

1 Sunil Gavaskar
2 Desmond Haynes
3 Greg Chappell
4 Viv Richards
5 Graeme Pollock
6 Garfield Sobers
7 Ian Botham
8 Alan Knott
9 Richard Hadlee
10 Dennis Lillee
11 Shane Warne

'Quite simply the most staggering cricketer of all time. A brilliant left-handed batsman, left arm over-the-wicket fast bowler, unorthodox left-arm spinner and brilliant fielder.'
Henry Blofeld
on Gary Sobers

The TMS Team – pictured above in 1991 – chose Sunil Gavaskar, left, to open with Desmond Haynes, whose usual West Indies opening partner Gordon Greenidge was 'selected' as 12th man

The No 1 player of the
century: Don Bradman

313

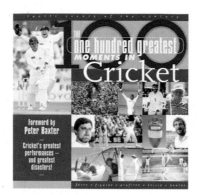

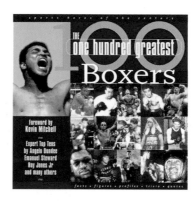

Available now from Generation Publications

(020 7403 0364)